William Allen

Quaker Friend of Lindfield

1770 – 1843

Margaret Nicolle

Copyright © Margaret Nicolle

William Allen, Quaker Friend of Lindfield 1770-1843

ISBN 0-9541301-0-3

First published 2001
by
Margaret Nicolle
Longmead
The Wilderness
Lindfield
West Sussex
RH16 2LB

Every effort has been made to trace and acknowledge any existing copyright owners.

All rights reserved.
No part of the book to be reprinted or reproduced,
in any form or by any means, without permission.

smallprint
35 Silver Birches
Haywards Heath
West Sussex RH16 3PD

William Allen.
(Library of the Religious Society of Friends in Britain.)

The Author

Margaret Nicolle graduated in history at King's College, London before taking the University's Diploma in Education and proceeding to a teaching career. Her other interests include music, art, travel and environmental issues. She has resided in Lindfield for over thirty years and is currently Chairman of Lindfield Parish Council.

Acknowledgements

I wish to acknowledge the friendly assistance given to me by Lorraine Jones, Assistant Curator at the Museum of the Royal Pharmaceutical Society of Great Britain, the librarians at the Library of the Religious Society of Friends in Britain, especially Joanna Clark and Peter Daniels, and Brian York, Archivist at the British and Foreign School Society (BFSS) Archives Centre, Brunel University. I am grateful for the use of books and records held at the above mentioned Museum and libraries. I also acknowledge the assistance of Martin Hayes, Principal Librarian of Local Studies, West Sussex County Council Library Service, Richard Childs, County Archivist at the West Sussex Record Office, and Eileen Maughan, Archivist for GlaxoSmithKline. A special debt is owed to Professor Roy Bridge who made invaluable comments and criticisms of the entire manuscript.

It is not possible to mention everyone individually but I appreciate the help given to me by the librarians at the Wellcome Trust and at the Worthing and Haywards Heath Libraries. I am grateful for the assistance of Rachel Anscombe Munn and Christine Irwin in typing my manuscript, to the reviewers of my book and to my proof-readers. Finally, thanks to my husband, Bill, whose shared love of history made him happy to listen and debate.

Dedicated to my father
Albert Ireland Burrows (Bunny)
and to his friend and colleague
James Scott Wilkie
almost a second father;

also to the people of Lindfield
and all who have known and loved
this Sussex village and its history.

"What is written without effort is in general read without pleasure." [1]

Samuel Johnson (1709-1784)

Foreword

Margaret Nicolle's meticulous and authoritative account of the career of the well known Quaker William Allen will be of interest not merely to devotees of local and social history. It also throws light on court politics, drawing attention as it does to Allen's contacts with members of the British Royal Family. Even more significant are its insights into the international scene through Allen's involvement with the Emperor Alexander I (in his 'humanitarian' phase). Allen himself attended the Congress of Verona in 1822 along with Alexander, Wellington and Metternich when the future of the slave trade was on the agenda.

The Village of Lindfield, Sussex, will be indebted to her for tracing the legacy of its distinguished former resident.

F. R. BRIDGE,
Professor of Diplomatic History,
University of Leeds.

Preface

I have been aware for some time that there is little readily available information about the life and work of William Allen whom Helena Hall described as 'Lindfield's greatest benefactor'. As my reading progressed I became anxious to reassess the character and achievements of a man whom Victorian biographers and also Helena Hall tended to eulogise. Books with titles such as 'The Spitalfields Genius' by J. Fayle, (an expression later used by Helena Hall) made me keen to check the facts, put William Allen into his contemporary context and allow modern readers to make their own judgements. Naturally I had hoped to find plenty of primary source material from the original diaries, which Allen kept meticulously throughout his life. Imagine my disappointment on finding that the original diaries were no longer intact. It would seem sacrilege to tamper with diaries today, but Victorians had no such scruples. In his will Allen consigned his manuscripts to his late wife's niece Lucy Bradshaw and his friend Susanna Corder and, in fairness to them, he instructed them to destroy whatever, in their judgement, was not likely to be profitable to society. Once *The Life of William Allen* with selections in three volumes from his correspondence had been edited by his niece and published by C. Gilpin (1846), the original diaries 'hacked about and in tatters' were destroyed.[2] The complete diaries might have provided a useful insight into his personal relationships or his attitude to James Mill,[3] for sometime a regular contributor to *The Philanthropist* and to Jeremy Bentham and his followers the Benthamites.[4]

In search of William Allen –
Quaker,
chemist,
social reformer
and
Lindfield benefactor.

I expect to pass through this world but once –
Any good thing therefore that I can do,
Or any kindness that I can show to any fellow creature,
Let me do it now –
Let me not defer or neglect it,
For I shall not pass this way again.

    Attributed to Stephen Grellet [5], French Quaker.

Contents

	Page
The Author	6
Acknowledgements	6
Foreword	8
Preface	9
Table of Contents	11
List of Illustrations	12
Introduction	15
Chronology of William Allen's Life 1770 – 1843	20

Chapter 1:	Early Life and Education	22
	Efforts at Self-improvement	22
	The Influence of Quakerism on the Character of William Allen	25
	His Scientific Interests	28
Chapter 2:	William Allen's Humanitarian Interests	36
Chapter 3:	Opposition to the Slave Trade	42
Chapter 4:	Allen as a National and 'International' figure	46
Chapter 5:	Marriages and Family Life	52
Chapter 6:	Political and Personal Satire and Brief Description of 1827 Caricatures	59
Chapter 7:	Contemporary Educational Views	68
Chapter 8:	Allen's Involvement with Lancaster, Owen and the Fleetwood House School	72
Chapter 9:	Rural Communities – Social and Economic Conditions	85
Chapter 10:	The Lindfield Connection – Why Lindfield?	87
Chapter 11:	The Establishment of Schools of Industry and a Boarding School in Lindfield and their Success	90
Chapter 12:	Allen's Plan for District Schools	106
Chapter 13:	The Anglican Alternative – The Lindfield Schools 1832-2000	111
Chapter 14:	The Lindfield Allotments	116
Chapter 15:	Assessment of William Allen	140
Bibliography		146
Notes and References		148
Index		156

Illustrations

Cover picture:

    William Allen, photographed from lithograph from drawing by T. F. Dicksee. © Library of the Religious Society of Friends, London.

                                                                                Page

William Allen	5
Silhouettes of Margaret and Mary Allen	22
William Allen branch of the Allen family	23
The Old Plough Court Pharmacy, 1715	24
Extract from laboratory calculation book	32
William Allen's Certificate of Membership of the Pharmaceutical Society of Great Britain	34
Analytical Laboratory, Old Plough Court Pharmacy	35
Manufacturing Laboratory, Old Plough Court Pharmacy	35
Soup Kitchen, 53 Brick Lane, Spitalfields	38
Peter Bedford, silk manufacturer and two young thieves	40
The Anti-Slavery Convention, 1840	44
Medallion of Emperor Alexander I	48
Extract from a William Allen letter illustrating the use of the diplomatic bag	50
Series of caricatures:	
Sweet William and Grizzell [sic]	61
Willy The Lion, Insulted By Asses	63
Untitled caricature	64
Yea Verily The Spirit Moveth or	
The Wedding Day Of William and Grizzell [sic]	65
The Attraction Of Gravity	67
Portrait of Joseph Lancaster	73
Portrait of Robert Owen	77
Caricatures (in colour):	
The Modern Alchemist	81
Racing Intelligence or Money Makes The Mare To Go	81

Four colour illustrations from the Quaker Tapestry Scheme*:
  John Bellers   82
  Elizabeth Fry   82
  William Allen   83
  The Slave Trade   83
Caricature (in colour):
  Sweet William and Grizzell [sic]   84
Resolution to open an Anglican Sunday School   89
Friends Meeting House, Ship Street, Brighton   90
Letter written by Allen about the Lindfield School   92
Extract of 1874 Ordnance Survey Map   94
Curricula provided in certain Schools of Industry   96
Title Page for the History of Richard Macready   99
The 55th Square – The Lindfield Schools   109
Presentation copy of Linfield [sic] British Schools Jubilee 1875
  Life of William Allen   113
Memorial Board to William Allen   114
Pelham Place Cottages (formerly the workshops and dormitories)   115
The former Schoolmaster's House – Little Pelham   115
The Rural Colony on Gravely [sic] Estate   121
Gravelye Lane about 1914   122
Outline plan of a cottage and farmyard   125
Two illustrations of Gravelye Cottages Lindfield c.1908   127
Gravelye Cottages Lindfield c.1912   128
Aerial view of Mid Sussex Laundry showing allotments at rear; late 1920's 128
William Allen's Cottage, Gravelye Lane   136
William Allen's house in Gravelye Lane as it is today   137
The last cottage, 1950s   138
Portrait of William Allen, from a photograph,
  held by the Library of the Religious Society of Friends in Britain,
  of an engraving by P. Elie Bovet of Geneva, 1823.   145

---

* The Quaker Tapestry – community embroidery for story telling and communication. Made by 4,000 people from 15 countries.
  Further information about the 77 panels of embroidery can be obtained from:
  The Quaker Tapestry Exhibition Centre, Friends Meeting House, Stramongate, Kendal, Cumbria LA9 4BH, UK. Phone 01539 722975.
  Open to the public from spring to early winter every year.
  Website: www.quaker-tapestry.co.uk   Email: info@quaker-tapestry.co.uk

Introduction

Quakerism

William Allen's religious faith was very obviously a driving force throughout his life, so some explanation of Quakerism, its history and faith seems appropriate. In seventeenth-century England a number of religious sects such as Presbyterians, Independents, Congregationalists, Baptists and Quakers questioned the authority of the established Church of England. Initially it was hoped that reforms would come from within. George Fox, son of a weaver, came to believe that the seed of God lay in the heart of all men waiting to be discovered by the individual. His insistence on personal experience, as opposed to rigid biblicism or reliance on an external source of spiritual authority, led to his arrest in Derby in 1650. He was charged and imprisoned under the Blasphemy Act. During his eight-hour examination of Fox, Justice Bennett coined the name Quakers for the followers of George Fox who had bidden the magistrates 'tremble (quake) at the name of the Lord.'[6] Another source states that it was Fox himself who said 'I tremble for no man but the Lord.' When he was due to be released, he was offered a captaincy in the Commonwealth army. He replied that he 'lived in the virtue of that life and power that took away the occasion of all wars.' No persuasion could make him change his mind and he was returned to prison 'amongst thirty felons in a lousy, stinking low place in the ground without any bed.'[7] In all he spent nearly a year in prison. In 1994 Larry Ingle rewrote the story of George Fox using contemporary sources rather than relying too heavily on Fox's *Journal* written late in life with the benefit of hindsight. 'Fox was not a pacifist in the modern sense that he utterly rejected participating in all wars and violent conflicts. He recognised that someone must wield the sword against evildoers.' Circumstances gradually led him to adopt 'survival tactics' in order to 'preserve his sect and convince the authorities of its peaceful intent.' The full Quaker Peace testimony, which influenced the lives of many Quakers, took time to evolve.[8] Fox refused to recognise one code of manners for the rich and one for the poor. He would use the same plain language for all and bare his head before God alone. In the Puritan tradition, plainness of dress, temperance in food and drink were upheld. He wanted fair dealing and honesty in trade, justice in the courts and high ideals in education and family life.

The Growth of the Quakers

The Quakers' outspoken attacks on the paid ministry and church institutions, their non-payment of tithes, refusal to honour magistrates by removing hats, refusal to perform military service and refusal to take the Oath of Abjuration,[9] made them a thorn in the side of the authorities – provincial magistrates, army officers, clerics of the Church of England, members of Parliament. C. Fleet, in his book *Glimpses of our Sussex Ancestors*, relates various local incidents which serve to illustrate the sort of persecution suffered. He quotes for example a contemporary account from Lewes in 1658: 'For these two yeares there hath been fire thrown in among friends severall times to the danger of fireing the house, some friends receiving much wrong by the fire and they also have thrown in water, dirt and cowdung upon friends in their meeting and have broke the glass windows very much and have beaten friends as they have passed to their meetings.'[10]

The magistrates' records for Chichester, Arundel and Horsham show commitments to prison and fining for non-attendance at court and non-payment of tithes.

The Clarendon Code – a series of laws passed in 1662 against all Dissenters – made life difficult for the Quakers. The use of the English Prayer Book and regular public worship was demanded.[11] The Corporation Act made it difficult for non-Anglicans to serve on public bodies.[12] The Conventicle Act of 1664 made it an offence for any person over sixteen to be present at a religious meeting at which five or more were present beyond the household. Penalties ranged from fines and imprisonment to (on a third offence) a £100 fine or seven years transportation to any plantation in the American Colonies except Virginia or New England. The Five-Mile Act prevented ministers from teaching or even living within five miles of any corporate or Parliamentary borough unless they swore never to attempt any alteration in the church or state. Up to the passing of the Toleration Act of 1689 over 450 Quakers died in prison and 15000 suffered various legal sentences. Others such as William Penn sought freedom in the New World, where he founded the colony of Pennsylvania in 1681. Quakers came from all classes except the aristocracy and totally unskilled labourers, but the sense of personal responsibility and commitment, engendered in their faith, appealed particularly to the middle classes. As a result of the harsh laws, the Quakers often withdrew a little and became a separate body distinguished by what most perceived to be a peculiar form of worship and distinctive mode of dress and speech characterised by the use of 'thee' and 'thou'.

Quaker Faith

This has changed little since its early beginnings. It is not possible to define Quaker faith by creed or dogma. There is no singing of hymns or repeating of set prayers. At the meetings, any one can speak who feels sincerely moved to do so. Fundamental is the Quaker doctrine of the Inner Life. Every meeting is held on the basis of the silent communion of the spirit, in which there is opportunity for spoken ministry arising spontaneously from the life of the meeting – by any man or woman, young or old. There is something of God in all people: 'God's light is in us all waiting to be discovered.' The Bible, though well read, shares authority with other potential sources of inspiration such as the direct illumination that can enlighten every man or woman. Meetings to worship God and await his word are essential to Quaker faith and practice although the inward seed can work in a solitary person. At times meetings can be totally silent. Quaker Faith and Practice 1994 repeats the words of 1884: 'We highly prize silent waiting on the Lord in humble dependence on him. We esteem it to be a precious part of spiritual worship and trust that no vocal offering will ever exclude it from its true place in our religious meetings.'

Quaker Organisation

At first meetings were held in Quaker homes. From a series of ad hoc meetings between 1667-69 George Fox created a regular structure of monthly area and quarterly county (later regional) meetings, with Yearly Meeting held for all members drawn from different parts of the country. The organisation remains the same today. There was and is no formal salaried clergy and all members share responsibility for pastoral care, but elders and overseers are also appointed by the members. The elders are concerned with spiritual welfare and the right holding of meetings. It is their task to encourage the preparation of mind and spirit and the study of the Bible. Overseers encourage Friends to attend meetings, welcome strangers, look after the children and visit Friends, assisting them with their everyday problems. A meeting closes after the elders have shaken hands. Travelling to visit and worship with Friends is valued. William Allen was on his way from London to a meeting in Brighton when he passed through Lindfield, Sussex – an incident that was to be of considerable significance to the village.

Quaker Peace Testimony

If there is something of God in all people, more can be accomplished by appealing to this capacity for love and goodness in others and ourselves than can be hoped for by threatening punishment or retaliation if people act badly. Quakers do not ignore the existence of evil but instead of weapons that kill they prefer 'weapons of the spirit', such as love, truth and non-violence. William Allen believed so firmly that war was wrong he turned down what would have been a very lucrative contract to undertake the supply of drugs for the Russian Military Services. The Royal Society obituary notice stated: 'To his honour he resisted a temptation the value of which it would be difficult to estimate.' Quakers were conscientious objectors in both world wars.

Education

Quakers, like all Puritan dissenters (later collectively known as Nonconformists), were excluded from universities by the existence of religious tests not abolished until the 1870s. The Quakers, like other sects, established their own schools. Medicine at that time could be entered through apprenticeship to an apothecary,[13] followed very often by studies at Edinburgh or Leyden, where there were no religious tests (the Quaker John Fothergill,[14] a foremost physician of his day, followed this course). A number of Quakers became prominent scientists, such as John Dalton[15] and William Allen.

Involvement in Trade and Industry

Although Quakers were excluded from the professions, Nonconformist religious principles upholding steady labour in a calling, economy and simplicity in private lives (the Protestant work ethic) encouraged them to turn to trade and industry. To mention but a few names, there were the iron masters of Coalbrookdale – the Darbys, goldsmiths such as John Freame, cloth manufacturers such as the Guerneys of Norfolk and Backhouses of Darlington, Joseph Fry of Bristol – founder of the first great Quaker Cocoa firm, William Cockworthy and Richard Champian significant in the development of the Bristol China Clay industry. Quakers such as George Stephenson and Edward Pease were involved in the development of railways – the Stockton to Darlington line was opened in 1825. Quakers played a prominent part in the development of corn-milling, foodstuffs, brewing and banking.

A Pressure Group for Social, Economic and Political Reform

During the seventeenth century persecutions, Meeting for Sufferings was set up to co-ordinate attempts to alleviate oppression. By the early nineteenth century, this London gathering of Quakers included country members now able to attend by rail transport. Meeting for Sufferings discussed such matters as slavery, relief work, unemployment, penal affairs, race relations and peace. William Allen was a member of Meeting for Sufferings. In the early nineteenth century there was increasing concern about poor living and working conditions. A growing number of people of all religious backgrounds, including many Quakers, became involved in philanthropic causes. Indeed, the expression came to be coined: 'Scratch a Quaker and there is a radical underneath.'

William Allen 1770-1843

Chronology

1770 29th August. Born, in Spitalfields, London, eldest son of Job and Margaret Allen. Father, who came from Scrooby, Nottinghamshire was a Quaker silk merchant who worked in Spitalfields. William Allen was a pupil at a dame school, then a Quaker school in Rochester.

1784 Prevented by religion from attending university entering the legal profession or taking municipal office, he was apprenticed to his father's business.

1792 Accepted a clerkship in Joseph Gurney Bevan's chemical establishment at Plough Court, London. Soon entered St Thomas' Hospital as a physician's pupil. Elected a member of the Chemical and Physical Societies at Guy's Hospital.

1794 When Bevan retired, formed a partnership first with Samuel Mildred then with Luke Howard (1797).

1796 Married Mary Hamilton from Redruth Cornwall at a Tottenham Meeting. The marriage lasted less than a year as Mary died in 1797, five days after the birth of a daughter also called Mary (1797-1823).

1802 Began lectures on chemistry and physics at Guy's Hospital.

1803 Elected a President of the Physical Society at Guy's.

1804 Gave a course of lectures on natural philosophy at the Royal Institution at the invitation of Sir Humphrey Davy.

1805 Married Charlotte Hanbury (d.1816).

1806 Elected a Fellow of the Royal Society (founded in 1662, the oldest scientific body in Great Britain). Involved in setting up the Geological Society.

1810 Appointed clerk to Meeting for Sufferings.

1811 Started 'The Philanthropist' magazine. Until 1818 editor of this monthly journal.

1812 Both William and Charlotte became Quaker elders.

1814 Elected a Member of the Council of the Royal Society.

1813 Visit of Emperor Alexander I to a Friends Meeting in London. Allen involved with Robert Owen in the New Lanark concern.

1818 Visit with Elizabeth Fry and Cornelius Hanbury to Newgate.

1818 John Thomas Barry became a partner in William Allen and Company.

1820 Became a Quaker minister.

1822 Daughter Mary married Cornelius Hanbury at Devonshire House Meeting in Bishopsgate Street.

1823 Birth of a son, William Allen Hanbury, to Mary and Cornelius. Mary died in childbirth.

1824 Allen discussed with the Earl of Chichester, Lord of the Manor of Lindfield, the acquisition of land in Lindfield on which to build an industrial school. Daniel Bell Hanbury and Cornelius Hanbury admitted to partnership. Company became Allen, Hanburys and Barry.[16]

1825 School started with workshops and dormitories on Black Hill, Lindfield. John Smith MP purchased 100 acres of land at Gravelye, Lindfield for 18 cottages with allotments.

1826 Married widow Mrs Grizell Birkbeck.

1841 Pharmaceutical Society organised. Allen appointed President of the Council.

1843 William Allen died December 30th at Gravelye Cottage, Lindfield. Buried at Stoke Newington in the Friends Burial Ground.

Chapter 1
Early Life and Education

Efforts at Self-Improvement

The eldest son of Quaker parents, Job and Margaret Allen, William was born on August 29th, 1770 in Stewart Street, Spitalfields. As a silk merchant with a business in Spitalfields, Job Allen prospered. William attended a dame school[1] and then a Quaker boarding school in Rochester.

MARGARET ALLEN,
NÉE STAFFORD
1747—1830.

MARY ALLEN,
Only daughter of WM. ALLEN, *of Plough Court,*
Married CORNELIUS HANBURY, *and died after the birth*
of her first child, WM. ALLEN HANBURY.
1797—1823.

Silhouettes of mother Margaret Allen and his daughter Mary.
Leaves from the Past: The Diary of John Allen ed. Clement Young Sturge.
(Library of the Religious Society of Friends in Britain.)

As the eldest child and business successor, it was assumed that on leaving school he would enter the silk trade. In 1784 he reluctantly became an apprentice in the counting house of his father's silk mill, feeling that it was his filial duty to do so. A sense of family obligation and the influence of his mother kept him at the family business until 1792, when he accepted a clerkship in Joseph Gurney Bevan's chemical establishment at Plough Court, off Lombard Street in the City of London. As he had long wished to be a scientist this move provided a welcome opportunity. The family heart-

THE WILLIAM ALLEN BRANCH OF THE ALLEN FAMILY

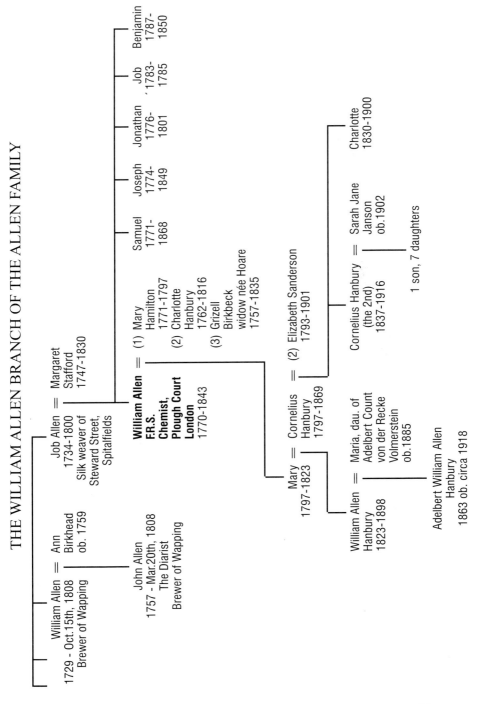

The Old Plough Court Pharmacy, 1715.
(Through a City Archway. The Story of Allen and Hanburys.)

searching and anguish is revealed by a sentence written eighteen years later by his mother: 'It was a bitter cup to me to part with thee.'[2]

Allen was quick to help himself. He taught himself shorthand to facilitate note taking. He was anxious to fill any gaps in his academic education. 'A grand object with me is to perfect myself in the study of medicine also in Latin.'[3] Other subjects of study were Chemistry, Botany, Physics, Astronomy and Natural Philosophy. He worked hard to achieve his objectives. He rose at 4 or 5 am. After Bible reading and attending to correspondence, the remaining time before breakfast was devoted to study – French, German and, at one stage, Russian. In drawing he engaged the services of a Master and it seems likely that much later he designed the Lindfield Allotment cottages.

A few years later he began the study of Algebra and when on holiday was 'pretty busily engaged in taking angles and in calculating them which has considerably improved me in trigonometry.'[4] He endeavoured always to be systematic. In July 1796 he wrote: 'I do think that I should get on with much less embarrassment if I arranged my matters in the morning and plodded through them one by one keeping my whole attention fixed to that with which I was occupied at the time.'[5] Little time was wasted. In July 1800 he wrote: 'Occupy every spare minute for standing jobs not infringing upon the fixed time for certain things. Much time is lost in desultory indecision. When this comes on catch up the first thing that comes to hand of those that must be done.'[6] In December 1800 he noted: 'Saved about 12 hours this week by early rising.'[7]

The Influence of Quakerism on the Character of William Allen

William Allen's religion was to be a guiding influence throughout his life. He wore the typical sober dress of the Quaker – yarn stockings, knee breeches, a distinctive cut of coat and, of course, the hat. Having lit his own fire (in his study), he would spend a quarter of an hour in prayer and a quarter of an hour in reading the Bible at the start of each day. He would regularly attend meetings for worship mid-week as well as Sundays and carry out a weekly review of his conduct and use of time. His earliest religious teaching was from his mother, to whom he was devoted. He was to keep some of her letters in his pocket book all his life. In his diary he wrote: 'I well remember the deep religious solicitude which my honoured and beloved mother felt for her children, how she used to collect us round her in her chamber when we very young and talk to us in terms adapted to our capacity, of the things which belong to the ever lasting kingdom of our Lord and Saviour Jesus Christ.'[8] She herself appears to have had little interest in anything outside her religion and home. His mother feared that his expanding interests might distract him from his own spiritual needs and goals: 'Thou art too much absorbed in study', she complained. At times she attempted to discourage him from all his activities, possibly with some effect. A reference in the diary which he studiously kept for most of his life states: 'The following great objects are enough for one man and I must resist all attempts to engage in more – the Overseership of Gracechurch Street monthly Meeting, Lancaster's concern, Spitalfields Local Association for the Poor, Spitalfields School, Philosophical Lectures, General Association for the Poor and the Bible Society.' [9]

Diary entries demonstrate the high moral principles, self discipline and sense of duty which guided his life. He engaged in frequent self-examination and constant self-criticism.

January 1788 (age 17 years):

> 'Experienced some degree of comfort in striving against evil thoughts.' [10]

(Did the diary editors expunge a few sentences?)

The work at his father's silk mill was not congenial to him:

> 'Morning – very much perplexed with my work but resolved to exert myself in it today and report consequence. Evening – the consequence was that I got forwarder in it than for several days past.' [11]

A sense of duty is also apparent when he was appointed a Quaker overseer in 1811:

> 'Though conscious of my unfitness for it, I was afraid to refuse lest I should shrink from a duty and thereby bring greater spiritual poverty upon myself. My prayer is to be preserved from doing any harm – if I can do no good. O for a grain of true faith.'

1793 diary review:

> 'I have attended some of Higgin's lectures,[12] learnt something of shorthand and the new system of Chemistry and instituted a plan for my future studies.'

Three weeks later he wrote:

> 'Beware lest Chemistry and Natural Philosophy usurp the highest seat in thy heart.'

On October 25th 1797, he wrote:

> 'My mind was much affected this afternoon with a sense of an invisible power having preserved me from the great dangers which ardent desire for knowledge had thrown in my way.'

Less than a month later he states:

'Rather comforted this morning – it seemed to open my view, with respect to my great attraction to natural science, that when I felt it strong and likely to get the ascendancy, it would by my duty to indulge less in it, abridge the time devoted to it and fast from it.'

He does not say what he did with the time he consequently saved! [13]

His early diary reveals his regrets for his impatience, his resolve to 'spend no time unprofitably' and his meditation on the 'happy state of those who are led and guided by the spirit of Truth.' He wrote:

'May I be favoured to guard against peevishness, even when just cause, or what appears so, is given and also to strive against foolish lightness.' [14]

A 1796 diary entry reads :

'Resolved to endeavour by all means to acquire more firmness of character and more indifference to what even my nearest friends may think of me – in the pursuit of what I believe to be right – to avoid every species of craft or dissimilation – to spend more time in my own room, in reading and retirement.' [15]

He resolved to be careful to avoid egotism –

'I feel great self-contempt when I detect myself in doing anything to be seen of men.'

He was always a harsh critic of himself –

'I am certainly a very poor, weak creature much wanting in firmness and strength of mind, vain, abounding in self-love and very indolent.'

'Beware of a spirit of pride in forming a judgement of things which through ignorance, thou art not qualified to judge. It is safer to consider well and not be hasty in judgement.'

'I must learn to bear with and still love my brethren even when I think they are acting upon mistaken principles.' [16]

'Too much resented a reproof – a sure sign that I needed it and had too high an estimation of self.' [17]

It is not surprising that at times someone who set himself high moral standards should have moods of despondency.

1812, 2nd month: [18]

'Still under depression; my little stock of faith almost exhausted and yet I can humbly say, in the multitude of things which harass my mind, the main object is the good of others – for this I have in great measure, given up my own gratification – for if instead of these things, my time were devoted to philosophical pursuits and experiments, to which I am so naturally prone, the path to honour and distinction stands fair before me. May the sacrifice be accepted above!' [19]

1814 Review:

'Faith and hope at a low ebb this week – discouraged by a feeling of my own weakness and assailed by fears.'

1821:

'In the latter part of the day I was sensible of too much irritability and was more shut up and reserved than is common.' [20]

According to Chapman-Huston and Cripps, 'he was almost pathologically sensitive and so emotional that, like Shelley, he was easily moved to tears and could be impatient when stressed.' [21]

A modern reader might find the diary sentiments self righteous, but they reveal Allen's efforts to control his own perceived character defects and uphold his Quaker beliefs.

He was quite prepared to state his views firmly on issues about which he felt strongly, as the letter he wrote to his Lindfield neighbours on the subject of Church Rates in 1839 clearly indicates:

'Address to the Parishioners of Lindfield.

Respected Friends. It is always painful to my feelings to be obliged to be engaged in differences with my friends and neighbours – but when matters of principle are in question, and particularly those connected with civil and religious liberty, I dare not shrink from avowing my sentiments and supporting those principles to the utmost of my power. I appeal to the liberal portion of the Church of England resident in this parish whether they think it right to compel their brethren to support forms of worship, to which they consistently object; and whether it is fair or consistent with common honesty to put their hands into the pockets of their dissenting brethren, for the support of their own particular forms and ceremonies of religion. I remain with best wishes for all my neighbours. Their sincere friend. William Allen. Gravely Cottage, Lindfield. 20th of ninth month, 1839.' [22]

His Scientific Interests

By the time William Allen was fourteen he was already displaying an interest in astronomy. Not having much money he acquired some cardboard, bought an eye-piece and an object glass and constructed a small telescope through which he could see the moon and the satellites of Jupiter – for the cost of one shilling and two pence. He remained an ardent astronomer all his life. A diary entry refers to him relaxing with his telescope on the roof of his house in Stoke Newington. His observations of the transits of the planets were later published.

As he was obviously a bright young man, Bevan marked him out for rapid promotion. He allowed him to attend lectures on science at St Thomas' Hospital and at Guy's Hospital. These opportunities were not given to the other assistants in the pharmacy – the skilled dispensers and chemical operators who worked a 12 hour day, lived in and earned £34 - £40 per annum.

A 1795 reference on his diary mentions that he practised among Guy's Hospital patients. 'Went to the hospital – received the thanks of a poor sick patient, which did me more good than a guinea fee.' [23] In 1798 he noted: 'I am making great progress in chemical experiments ... fused platina with oxygen on charcoal.' [24] He resolved to study pharmacy regularly and conducted two or three experiments weekly. With the formation of the Askesian Society, which met at Plough Court, the place became a gathering ground for all interested in science. Men such as John Dalton, Professor Berzelius, Humphrey Davy, Astley Cooper and Dr. William Babington attended. All were interested in scientific discussion and experiment. Each member was expected to produce a paper for reading and discussion upon some subject of scientific inquiry, and many of these papers were published afterwards in Tilloch's Philosophical Magazine. In February 1800 it was Allen's turn. His diary refers to 'Experiments on respiration'. 'We all breathed the gaseous oxide of azote (laughing gas).[25] It took a surprising effect upon me, abolishing completely at first, all sensation; then I had the idea of being carried violently upward in a dark cavern, with only a few glimmering lights. The Company said my eyes were fixed, face purple, veins in the forehead very large ... they were all much alarmed but I suffered no pain and in a short time came to myself.' [26]

Allen and his friend W. H. Pepys wrote a paper on their experiments 'On the Quality of Carbon in Carbonic Acid and the Nature of the Diamond', proving that diamond was pure carbon like charcoal and that the materials did not contain hydrogen as was previously thought. The Council of the Royal Society would have awarded the gold medal if the paper had been written by only one person. However, Allen was made a Fellow of the Royal Society.

In 1802 he began lectures on chemistry and physics at Guy's Hospital and he was to continue until 1826. An account of his lectures at Guy's exists and is quoted below:

'It was on January 10th, 1802, that Dr. Babington called at

Plough Court and offered Allen a partnership in his lectures on chemistry at Guy's Hospital. This visit was followed by Astley Cooper, who strongly advised Allen to accept the offer. Obviously such required earnest consideration and after consulting with J. G. Bevan, he agreed to Dr. Babington's suggestion and about a month later he gave his first lecture. He felt he says, low and anxious, but he got through, much to his satisfaction, although much distressed by the loud plaudits of the students, which began and ended the lecture. On the 16th March 1814, Allen gave a lecture at the Hospital on Earths and showed Iodine for the first time. In December 1816 ... Allen was lecturing both morning and evening and the new theatre was crowded. In a week's review in his diary he notes; "that the lectures are a great weight upon me and take up much time, yet I get through them satisfactorily and I understand that the pupils are greatly pleased". His subjects were always topical: he gave a lecture on the steam engine in 1817. The lectures were divided into two main sections: Physics, which were given in the evenings, and chemistry, which were given in the mornings:

PHYSICS		CHEMISTRY	
Subject	*No. of lectures*	*Subject*	*No. of lectures*
Astronomy	2	Acids	3
Electricity	5	Caloric	6
Galvanism	2	Combustibles	4
Hydraulics	2	Earths	4
Hydrostatics	5	Elements	1
Magnetism	1	Gases (Oxygen)	3
Mechanics	10	Gases (Hydrogen)	1
Optics	5	Gases (Azote)	1
Pneumatics	5	Organic Substances	2
		Salts	2

'There were a few lectures outside these categories such as those on compound engines and on clocks. The apparatus used to demonstrate these included Bevan's crane, steam engine and circular saw, model of crank, pile driver, Flint's model of windmill, millwork and parts of a watch.

'In the bicentenary number of *Guy's Hospital Gazette*, published in 1926, there is a very appreciative note on William Allen and the work he did at the hospital. He is alluded to as the Spitalfields' Genius.'

(Reproduced with the permission of Glaxo Wellcome plc.)

From 1803 to 1810, with Humphrey Davy's encouragement, Allen also lectured at the Royal Institution on similar subjects. In the winter of 1803-4 he delivered over 100 lectures, but by 1810 he had reduced the figure to one a week due to pressure of work. Two letters dated 1810 are of interest:

'My dear Allen. As you are a professor of Natural Philosophy at the Institution your name, of course, must appear in the list of lecturers. I hope you will contrive to give some lectures. Mr. Pond will take a considerable part of optics and mechanics. Perhaps you will give a few, six for instance, on Pneumatics and Hydraulics. But you must be governed by your own convenience; your time is too precious to be employed in any way that is not pleasant to you, and that does not coincide with your own views of utility. I hoped to have met you at Dr Babington's, on Saturday, but was disappointed. I trust you are quite well, and that you do not injure your health by your unceasing exertion to promote all good things. I am, my dear Allen, most sincerely yours, H Davy.'[27]

The finances of the Institution were not too satisfactory in 1810, as will be seen from this letter written by Allen to Sir Humphrey Davy:

'Dear Davy,
    It is not pleasant to me, to say much about money matters, but on looking over my accounts I find that the last settlement with the Royal Institution was up to the end of the year 1806, and that beside the amt. for Chemicals there is £105 due to me for 24 lectures begun near the close of 1806 and finished in 1807. If I were to charge interest, which I shall not, there would be due to me

Int. on 1807 and 1808 Accts.	£6.14.-
Do. 3 years on £105	£15.15.-
	£22. 9.-

So that I may fairly consider myself that sum out of pocket. I just mention this, not with a view that the managers should be urged on the subject, but in hopes that if a favourable opportunity occurred and the state of the funds would permit, that thou wouldst just remind them of the claim of.

Yours sincerely, Wm. Allen.

P.S. I leave the settlement of the last 9 lects. delivered this year entirely to the Managers.'[28]

Allen seems to have been active in the formation of the Royal Jennerian Institution as illustrated by two diary entries:

Extract from Plough Court laboratory calculation book, 1795-98. (Museum of the Royal Pharmaceutical Society of Great Britain.)

'First month 9th 1802, Joseph Fox invited me to meet Dr Jenner at his house and go from thence to the Physical Society at Guy's, a paper on cowpox being before the Society.' [29]

'Second month 17th 1803 I went to the London Tavern, between 11 and 12, to the meeting on cow pox. The report of the Committee was read and approved. I am appointed a member of the board of directors.' [30]

Jenner became the President. In eighteen months over 12,000 inoculations were done in London. Unfortunately internal disputes took place, Jenner resigned from the Board and the National Vaccine Establishment was formed in 1808 to take the place of the Institution, which however remains an example of the interest and enthusiasm of its members.

Some of his Quaker friends were concerned about all this scientific work. A diary entry reveals: 'Dear Mary Stacey felt a draught in her mind yesterday to call in and hand the word of exhortation – to be on my guard against the world's flattery and applause.' [31]

Allen was a member of the Linnaean Society, having started the study of Botany at thirty, and a founder member of the Astronomical Society and the Geological Society. In 1804 he became an honorary member of the Board of Agriculture and delivered lectures 'on wheel carriages, roads and the application of mechanical principles to agricultural instruments.' [32]

He was a very successful chemist and druggist.[33] The Plough Court pharmacy manufactured and sold drugs wholesale and retail to druggists, merchants and surgeons, both in London and in the colonies. It also sold surgical instruments and medical books. Bevan retired in 1794 and sold the business to Samuel Mildred who took Allen into partnership and renamed the business Mildred and Allen. Allen bought Mildred out in 1797 and a succession of partnerships took place with Luke Howard and then with members of the Hanbury family and with Thomas Barry. Allen's meticulous attention to everything can be seen in surviving ledgers much of them in Allen's own hand.

With the departure of Luke Howard in 1806, the nature of the business changed. Allen concentrated on galenicals (made of vegetable components) and on certain chemicals which were not required in bulk. The population of London doubled between 1800 and 1840 providing a ready demand for retail medicines. Home trade became sufficient, so transatlantic trade was allowed to dwindle. The firm gained a reputation for quality goods. Credit was tightened and blunt reminders were sent out when necessary! The turnover figures show how solid the business was in the period 1815 to 1845. However, 'Commercially the pharmacy at Plough Court lacked dynamism and avoided efforts at expansion, preferring to remain uneasily placed between manufacturing and retailing. This was partly due to the Quaker philosophy of its partners – for whom business was never an end in itself.'[34]

Allen was active on the committee appointed to take steps to oppose the Bill introduced in Parliament by the Associated Apothecaries, which threatened the position chemists and druggists then occupied as dispensers of medicines. In 1815 the Apothecaries Act was passed giving apothecaries the right to be recognised as medical practitioners. This did not in fact interfere with the claims of chemists and druggists to make up physicians' prescriptions and generally to carry on the practice of pharmacy. When the Medical Bill of 1841 did threaten the interests of chemists and druggists, William Allen and Jacob Bell helped to organise a famous meeting at the Crown and Anchor tavern in the Strand on April 15th 1841, and as chairman Allen moved the resolution which resulted in the formation of the Pharmaceutical Society of Great Britain. He was appointed the first President of the Council – recognition of his standing as a scientist of distinction in what has been described as the 'golden age of chemistry' and no mean achievement for someone with a limited formal education.

*William Allen's membership certificate for the Pharmaceutical Society of Great Britain. June 1st, 1841. Designed by H. P. Briggs RA.
(Museum of the Royal Pharmaceutical Society of Great Britain.)*

*Analytical Laboratory of the Old Plough Court Pharmacy.
(Through a City Archway. The Story of Allen and Hanburys.)*

*Manufacturing Laboratory of the Old Plough Court Pharmacy.
(Museum of the Royal Pharmaceutical Society of Great Britain.)*

Chapter 2
William Allen's Humanitarian Interests

Allen was certainly not alone in his awareness of the social problems of his time. The social costs of industrialisation had been considerable – poor housing, bad living conditions, and long hours of work. Feelings were expressed in different ways: self-help co-operatives to provide better food, early trade union activity and the peaceful and violent protests of the Chartists with their demands for political representation for the working classes.

The Industrial Revolution led to increasing economic and political power for the middle class or 'middling classes' – manufacturers, merchants, bankers and other professional groups. Greater influence was exerted over government policy – either directly after the Great Reform Act of 1832 or indirectly as extra parliamentary pressure groups working through voluntary societies, special committees and by the use of tracts, journals and newspapers. Social reformers worked long and hard to achieve their ends, often in the teeth of vested interests: witness the Factory Acts of 1833, 1844, and 1847 and the long struggle for the Emancipation of Slaves in the British Empire. Both the 1807 Abolition of the British Slave Trade Act and the 1833 Emancipation Act, which formally ended slavery within the British Empire, were passed in spite of the powerful West Indian vested interests.

A wide cross-section of people, with different political and religious views, was interested in social reform. Allen sometimes referred to them as 'friends of humanity'. There were Whig leaders such as Holland, Whitbread and Brougham, free thinking radicals such as Bentham, Anglican Evangelicals, Dissenters – Methodists, Congregationalists, Baptists and Quakers and a few educated leaders of the workmen. The Evangelicals tended to be from the upper and middle classes. They included a highly organised group of well placed laymen known as the Clapham Sect; William Wilberforce, Granville Sharp, Lachary Macaulay and James Stephens were Evangelicals. Social reform was an expression of their Christian commitment. Wilberforce published an important religious journal – *The Christian Observer* – in which the subject matter ranged from the strict observance of the Sabbath to attacks on slavery. The Benthamites argued that old customs and rules should be tested by reason. Thinking men should ask what is the usefulness of such things. The greatest happiness of the greatest number should be the guiding rule.

Although historians now dispute the old view that the government pursued a laissez faire policy, nevertheless the scope of state action was often limited and not assisted by the contemporary belief in self-help. Social reformers had a real role to play in forwarding humanitarian actions. Although small in numbers, Quakers and Unitarians often had a disproportionate influence as active members of reform committees and Philosophical Societies. In the early 1900s Max Weber suggested a causal link between 'the Protestant ethic' and 'the spirit of capitalism'. He argued that there was a direct connection between the economic development of the Protestant world and the doctrinal attitudes of its churches. He was thinking largely of the Reformation period but he also suggested an eighteenth century link.[1] In the 1920s R. H. Tawney's book *Religion and the Rise of Capitalism* appeared. Tawney argued that the crucial point was not the Reformation but the emergence of Puritan sects in the late sixteenth century and especially the seventeenth century. After 1660 Presbyterians, Congregationalists, Baptists, Unitarians and Quakers took a large place in the ranks of entrepreneurs. Work was an end in itself, Labour and enterprise was for the service of God. Yet such views have been criticised. Protestant sects had a very cautious approach to money making and it was argued that ideas of thrift and diligence applied to personal consumption not to an aggressive work ethic. Even so, Ian Bradley's view is that 'Evangelicalism was to do for the rising English Middle Classes of the early nineteenth century what Calvinism had done for the emerging bourgeoisie of Europe nearly 300 years earlier. It gave them a creed, a confidence and a common consciousness and purpose.'[2] There was a call to 'seriousness' – an emphasis on hard work, plain living, moral propriety, respectable family life.

David McClelland in *The Achieving Society*, 1961 writes of the psychological needs of the individual rather than an aggressive work ethic. An individual might be motivated by a sense of 'belonging', a desire for recognition, friendship and need for order and need for achievement.[3]

In the case of Allen, some of his social work, such as his early trips abroad, appears to have been undertaken at the wish of the Gracechurch meeting. However, much of his social work was an expression of his own concerns.

Voluntary societies became an integral part of the British way of life. In spite of differences of religion and class, success was often achieved. In his account of the Spitalfields Soup Society Allen wrote: 'Here Dissenters and Churchmen, forgetting their little differences of opinion in other respects, unite cordially together in the work of Christian benevolence.'[4] Although the same philanthropists often appeared in different committees, Allen was perhaps sometimes blind to underlying tensions. The Radicals distrusted the Evangelical Movement because of its Tory associations and its tendency to defend the class structure. William Cobbett in the *Weekly Register* attacked Wilberforce for his apparent preference for West Indian slaves when there were white wage slaves in the mills of Northern England. Underlying suspicions and the Church of England's fear of losing influence led to the establishment of sectarian schools.

The Wide Scope of Allen's Humanitarian Interests

An extract from Allen's diary dated 1811 reveals some of the diversity of his social concerns: 'Third month, 5th To Devonshire House to meet committee on subscriptions for British prisoners in France.' 6th 'Three o'clock, Borough Road to meet Duke of Gloucester etc (the school).' 7th 'Capital Punishment Committee at four – full attendance.' 8th 'Thatched House Tavern, about two. Lancaster's Committee, Duke of Bedford present; good attendance.' [5]

Poverty at home was one of the issues which Allen attempted to address in his own local way. He was a pioneer in the formation of soup societies. In 1795, according to an account of conditions in Spitalfields and its neighbourhood published by Allen in *The Philanthropist*, some thousands

Soup Kitchen, 53 Brick Lane, Spitalfields.
(The Library of the Religious Society of Friends in Britain.)

of industrious poor families were, at times, reduced to great misery and destitution from the stagnation of trade and the high price of provisions. In 1806 Patrick Colquhoun estimated that more than one million people were rate aided out of a total population of less than nine million. In Spitalfields starving hand-loom weavers were put out of work by advancing technology. William Allen and William Phillips formed a society for supplying soup at a penny a quart in Brick Lane, Spitalfields. Five boilers made over 3000 quarts daily – at a loss to the society of about £150 a week. Financial contributions came from sympathetic benefactors.

Allen was also a member of the Spitalfield Association for the relief of special cases among the industrious poor. With Peter Bedford he was involved in the distribution of food and clothing and family visitation. Allen as always organised everything from the price of meat to facilities for orderly queues in meticulous detail. He argued in *The Philanthropist* that relief should be in kind not cash: 'The object was not to support the poor in idleness but to enable them to bear up under their present difficulties until the government may have found the means of giving new spirit to our languishing commerce and thereby full employment to our industrious poor.' One way of assisting the poor was by the establishment of Penny Banks. In 1816 Allen noted in his diary: 'Charles Barclay, Charles Dudley and Robert Stevens met me at Plough Court on the subject of savings banks for the poor ... and we laid the first stone of the building.' [6]

The Penal Code meant that 160 offences were punishable by death. In 1808 Allen was a founder member of the Society for Diminishing Capital Punishment – a society which was to work closely with Sir Samuel Romilly. In 1813 Allen became involved in the Morgan case. The twenty-two year old Morgan crept in at the window of a house in Cardiff and stole a trifle. He was sentenced to be hanged. His friends appealed to Allen. The diary entries tell the story: '9th October Lord Sidmouth (Home Secretary) received me politely but seemed bent upon hanging the man at the instance of the judge.' Allen wrote a long letter to Sidmouth: '10th October Shall a person to whom be it remembered, society has failed in its duty by suffering him to grow up in ignorance, for the crime of stealing to the amount of a few shillings – be cut off in the prime of life ... suffer the very same punishment which you inflict upon him who has been guilty of the most barbarous murder?' [7]

On October 12th Allen went to Whitehall and had a long interview with Sidmouth on the Morgan case. A note from Sidmouth on the 15th advised that he had recommended to the Prince Regent that the sentence be commuted to transportation for life. In acknowledging this note Allen wrote: 'I

Peter Bedford, silk manufacturer and two young thieves. (Bishopsgate Library, Bishopsgate Institute.)

wish it were in my power to convince those who, from their situation and influence are able to give full effect to the measure, that *it is possible* to make arrangements for the education of every poor child in the kingdom at a very trifling expense for the public, upon some general plan in which good men of all descriptions might cordially unite. This would do more towards diminishing crime than all the penal statutes that could be enacted.' [8]

The Quakers were very much involved in these issues. In 1818 Quaker petitions organised by Joseph John Gurney demanded Capital Punishment only for the most serious crime. Allen was chairman almost to his death of the Society for the Abolition of Capital Punishment for crimes against property. There were also prominent non-Quaker colleagues working in this area such as Thomas Fowell Buxton and William Crawford. The pressure for reform gradually bore fruit, and from the 1820s the number of crimes carrying the maximum penalty was much reduced.

In 1815 Allen helped to found a society to investigate the causes of juvenile delinquency in the East End. His journal entry records this as follows: 'A very bad cold and hoarseness. African Institution at one; lasted till near five ... just had time to get a little dinner, and then had a large meeting on the subject of the gangs of depredators from 9 to 12 years of age, who infest the metropolis; they are estimated at from 600 to 700. Some of them have recently been capitally convicted at the Old Bailey, and received sentence of death. [It is not clear to what extent the sentences were carried out.] Peter Bedford and my nephew, C. Hanbury, have visited the parents of many of these children, and collected important facts. The meeting was very satisfactory, and we resolved to establish a society. I was much exhausted and very unwell.' [9] Allen accompanied Elizabeth Fry on some of her prison visits. The diary entry for February 8th 1818 states: 'Went with Elizabeth Fry to Newgate. About one hundred women prisoners were collected and they behaved in a most exemplary manner. E. J. Fry read the seventh chapter of Luke ... I also ventured to address them and I felt peace. We were all well satisfied with our visit.' [10]

Chapter 3
Opposition to the Slave Trade

Britain was involved in the slave trade from the mid-seventeenth century. Increasing numbers of black slaves lived in England and by 1706 slavery in England was legal. The Somerset Judgement by Lord Mansfield in 1772 made a significant ruling: namely that English law does not recognise slavery. However, it was going to prove a long hard battle to end the slave trade and slavery itself in the British colonies, such was the strength of the West Indian lobby of planters and merchants involved in the triangular trade route. The contemporary view of many people was that slavery and the slave trade, like pain in surgery or childbirth, were deplorable necessities. However, reformers began to express their views in print. John Wesley's *Thoughts on Slavery* appeared in 1774. In 1784 James Ramsay's book *An Enquiry into the Effects of Putting a Stop to the African Slave Trade and of Granting Liberty to the Slaves in the British Sugar Colonies* drew attention to the 'barbarous cruelty and oppression'. Thomas Clarkson's *Essay on the Slavery and Commerce of the Human Species* was published in 1786. The greatest champion of the Abolitionists was of course William Wilberforce. In common with many Quakers, Allen was very opposed to the 'horrid traffic – disgraceful to human nature and to my country in particular. When I reflect upon the tyranny and oppression exercised by my countrymen towards the poor Africans and the many thousands yearly murdered in the disgraceful slave trade I can but be a zealous opposer.'[1]

In 1783, together with Quakers such as the Frys, Gurneys and William Forster, 273 Friends in all, Allen signed the first petition against the slave trade, in support of William Wilberforce, Thomas Clarkson and Thomas Fowell Buxton. A committee was appointed by Meeting for Sufferings and 12,000 copies of a pamphlet entitled 'The Case of our Fellow Creatures, the Oppressed Africans' were circulated to people of influence. Quakers were to figure prominently in the anti-slavery movement. On April 18th 1791 Allen occupied a front seat in the gallery of the old House of Commons and listened for nearly four hours to Wilberforce's speech supporting his Bill for the abolition of the slave trade. He was not there for the conclusion of the debate on April 20th 1791 – 'This morning I went to know the fate of the business yet as I approached the house of my friend, my heart palpitated and I was almost afraid to knock at the door Clarkson told him – Ah William – we are beat – beat all to pieces – almost 2 to 1 against us. Nos. 163. Ayes 88.' (Such was the influence of the West Indian lobby of planters!).[2]

Allen's diary reveals that he worked with Wilberforce, Clarkson, Joseph Wood and Granville Sharp – 'March 1806 Attended the committee for the abolition of the Slave Trade at Wilberforce's house.'[3] Clarkson became a friend, as did Wilberforce although somewhat more distantly. 'I wish your religious principles and my own were more entirely accordant',[4] Wilberforce wrote to Allen on one occasion. Allen decided that one of the most effective ways to oppose the trade and, later, slavery itself was by ceasing to use those commodities procured by the labour of slaves. He therefore gave up the use of sugar (when Emperor Alexander I offered him a cup of sweetened tea on his visit to Russia in 1818 and was made aware of Allen's scruples, he ordered another cup to be brought!).[5]

After the 1807 Act abolished the British Slave trade, the problems facing freed slaves occupied him. As he commented in his diary on December 27th 1813: 'Much taken up, day after day, with examining witnesses on the state of Sierra Leone before a committee of the African Institution. I feel it is a duty to stand by the poor black settlers.'[6] (Sierra Leone became a home for emancipated slaves). Allen was a founder member and Director of this Institution. The aim of the Institution was to encourage legitimate trade in Africa and an education programme. Allen felt strongly that the Africans needed to be protected from a clandestine slave trade. His 1810 diary refers to the apprehending and fining of a Portuguese ship – the Commerio de Rio – that had on board handcuffs, iron shackles for feet and provisions for 600-800 slaves.[7]

Frequent attempts were made to persuade France, Portugal and Spain to abolish their Slave Trade. The Congress of Vienna in 1815 issued a declaration condemning the Slave Trade, but the declaration had no teeth and much traffic persisted. In 1817 Wilberforce wrote to Grenville on the subject of 'the unrestrained great and continually increasing Spanish Slave Trade or Trade under the Spanish flag.' The same year a treaty was in fact made with Spain allowing British ships to search suspect vessels for slaves. However, problems concerning rights of search appeared regularly on the agendas of the Congresses and ambassadors' meetings, which were a feature of the post Napoleonic wars. An Abolitionist Lobby always appeared, headed either by Clarkson or Allen who became good friends. Wilberforce himself did not travel abroad. At the Congress of Verona in 1822, Allen endeavoured to secure support for a meaningful abolition of the Slave Trade, but he was unable to make much progress. The French particularly were vehemently opposed to British proposals regarding the policing of the seas. Rights of search would violate the principle of freedom of the seas and infringe upon national sovereignty. The Duke of Wellington confessed to

Allen that he had not merely to consider what was desirable but what was practicable; that if the other powers outlawed the Slave Trade as piracy, how were they to act against France without going to war?

In the meantime, from 1807 little was done to improve conditions for slaves on the West Indian plantations despite a number of laws passed by Colonial Legislatures at the request of Westminster. There was no legal security against sale nor was a black able to testify against a white in court. It became increasingly clear to the reformers that further action was needed. In 1823 an Anti-Slavery Society was formed with Wilberforce, Fowell Buxton, Clarkson and Stephen Macaulay in the lead. The Quakers, who of course included Allen, petitioned Parliament to abolish Slavery in the British Empire. Abolition was finally achieved in 1833 and Allen's personal self denial came to an end..

In his final years Allen was chairman of the Annual Meeting of the Anti-Slavery Society. The artist Benjamin R. Haydon has portrayed the scene at the first meeting of the British and Foreign Anti-Slavery Society convention which met at the Freemasons Hall in 1840. Allen is clearly seen below an aged Clarkson who is making his concluding remarks as President.

The Anti-Slavery Society Convention, 1840, Benjamin Robert Haydon.
(By courtesy of the National Portrait Gallery, London.)

A liberated slave, now a delegate, is looking up at Clarkson with deep interest. The significance of the scene would not have been lost on the contemporary viewer. A freed African – Henry Beckford of Jamaica – is sitting by the intelligent Europeans in equality. On a personal note, Allen once rescued an ill-treated West Indian boy and sent him to school. Known as Black Tom, this emancipated slave remained in his service for many years.[8]

Chapter 4
Allen as a National and 'International' Figure

Allen made eight journeys abroad. These were no mean achievements considering the discomforts and general difficulties at that time. In the first issue of *The Philanthropist* in 1810 he argued 'that even the poorest, may render material assistance in ameliorating the conditions of man.' Not only a strong social conscience but also a deep conviction that he was doing his religious duty compelled him to make these trips. There is evidence that some of the journeys were directly encouraged by his Quaker brethren. Twice he acted as 'caretaker' and organiser for Elizabeth Fry and Elizabeth Robson. They wished to visit small colonies of converts, and inspect schools and prisons in Belgium, Holland and Switzerland. A journey to Ireland in 1820 was made on the invitation of Friends Yearly Meeting in Dublin. He was accompanied by his daughter Mary and the eminent French Quaker minister Stephen Grellet. They visited schools, asylums and a prison in Ireland. (Those interested in his journeys to Sweden, Norway, Finland, Turkey, the Crimea, Greece, Italy, Spain, France, Prussia and Hungary should look at earlier biographies in which his impressions of continental experiments in social reform are described.) Much time was spent visiting prisons, hospitals, poor houses and schools. One illustration must suffice – his comments on the educational reformer Pestalozzi after he visited his educational community at Yverdon in Switzerland in 1816 and 1817: 'The lively old man saluted me with two kisses, one on each cheek ... A spirit of harmony seemed to pervade the whole establishment. I was much pleased.' [1]

In his biography Fayle wrote enthusiastically about Allen's achievements: 'There was', he stated, 'scarcely a sovereign in Europe whom Allen did not visit. In spite of his Quaker peculiarities about the hat and the "thou", everyone saw at once that he was a true Christian gentleman, sacrificing money, time and home comforts disinterestedly for the sake of the human race everywhere.' [2] His enthusiasm and sincerity were obviously apparent.

Conditions of travel could be arduous. For example, in 1818 he had a tedious journey to Christiansand in Norway then a gruelling land journey to Christiania. Sometimes they were beaten by the roads and even six horses could not force the carriage along. On one occasion coach, men and horses are alike 'used up'. The passengers and coachmen were obliged to pass the night by the roadside. In the spring of 1819 he set off for Odessa and

Constantinople by way of Moscow. He travelled in a Kibitka – a primitive sledge or wagon covered with a hood of leather or cloth and drawn in this case by three horses. The course of the road was shown only by branches of pine struck in at certain distances and the snow drifts covered holes, which could be 4-10 feet deep. If the horses could not scramble out of the holes, everyone had to get out and put their shoulders to the sledge. If, when travelling at night, the shafts of the sledge broke, they were forced to creep back under their coverings and wait until daylight. The sledge, in spite of outriggers, was liable to tip them out when crossing the snow and ice of the Valdai Hills, on their way to Moscow. Sometimes, as at Novorogod, Allen slept on a wolf skin, as Russian landlords did not provide beds. Sometimes travel stopped and all were obliged to lie quietly by the roadside until daybreak.'[3]

Allen's firm beliefs gave him the confidence to speak and write freely. He had no hesitation in telling Emperor Alexander I of his concern about the extensive use of brandy by the poor and the corruption rife in all government departments. In Stockholm he had an interview with the King and presented an address on prison discipline, education and the management of the poor. He spoke to the King of Prussia on the sufferings of pacifists and the need for religious liberty for Quakers. He was not only concerned with the position of Quakers. He endeavoured to secure protection for other minority groups such as the Mennonites on the banks of the Dnieper. He also supported the cause of the Waldenses (the Protestants of Savoy). The diary notes that on the 'ninth month 27th 1823 went to Downing Street by appointment to meet George Canning' [the Foreign Minister]. Canning 'agreed to press for the relief of the Waldenses.'[4] Never one to waste opportunities, Allen states that he 'endeavoured to impress his mind in favour of the Greeks', then embroiled in conflict with their Turkish overlords.

His relationship with Emperor Alexander of Russia and his trips to Russia are of particular interest. He first met the Emperor when he visited London in 1814. Alexander was anxious to attend a Quaker meeting and Allen was charged with making the arrangements for this and subsequent visits to Friends' houses. He was one of the three leading Quakers chosen to present the Quaker address. An unusual friendship developed between Allen and the Emperor who it seems had a respect for Allen's character and religious sentiments. The Emperor was at the time leaning towards a mystical form of religion, and the Quietism inherent in Quakerism appealed to him. Discussions about the Holy Spirit, worship as an internal and spiritual experience, in which forms and ceremonies were secondary, appealed to him. Allen urged him to support the movement against the slave trade and explained the work of the British and Foreign School Society (BFSS) and the Bible Society. The Emperor invited him to visit Russia and advise him on social schemes.[5]

During their second continental journey which, incidentally, lasted eighteen months, Grellet and Allen visited Russia. Allen's diary reveals that in St Petersburg he was impressed by the lunatic asylum and hospital, but that his educational plans met with opposition. Many of the Russian nobles of the time were nervous about the consequences of bringing education to the masses. 'What I have suffered in endeavouring to convince some of this class, I think I shall never forget.'[6] In spite of this setback he and his English friends 'literally worked night and day to produce a selection of the scriptures for use in schools.' The Emperor was so pleased with it that he gave £1,450 for the cost of the first edition, and the selection was to be used in BFSS schools for many years.

Allen and Grellet spent a month in Moscow. Once they had delivered their letters of introduction to the civil, military and police authorities they were free to inspect schools, prisons and hospitals and report their findings

Medallion of Emperor Alexander I.
(Library of the Religious Society of Friends in Britain.)

to the Emperor. They visited 37 schools of different types – military, district, boarding, foundling, bourgeois, sectarian, Jewish, Islamic and deaf and also an orphanage. Not surprisingly, as in St Petersburg, the idea of educating the masses, including girls, did not meet with much favour amongst many of the gentry and those in government circles, and apparently a wary eye was kept on the Quakers by the authorities.

On the evening of February 10th 1819 the Emperor received Allen and Grellet. According to Allen's diary: 'We were shown in at the Emperor's private door, and conducted to the private staircase. There was not the least pomp; not a single soldier on the stair, and the servants had no sword nor any livery or uniform. The Emperor was in a small apartment, with a sofa in it, a table and chairs – the whole very neat and plain. He was dressed in a blue uniform, with gold epaulettes, he received us very kindly, and we were soon sensible of a renewal of those feelings which we had experienced when with him before ... he invited us to sit down ... no one was present but ourselves ... He loves vital religion ... we were about two hours with him. We heard afterwards that he drove off immediately to the Princess Mestchasky, we having told him that she had a copy of the Scripture lessons used in our schools in England.' [7] Topics discussed with Alexander included education in the Russian army, general philanthropic projects for Russia and world peace. When they had concluded their discussions they knelt and prayed. Allen was later elected an honorary member of the Imperial Academy of Sciences.

It is surprising in some ways to find Allen, on his third journey, present at the Congress of Verona in 1822. How did this come about? By then he was known and respected as a leading Quaker philanthropist. In addition to pressing for strong anti-Slave Trade measures he also wished to draw attention to the plight of the Greek refugees from the war against the Turks. He was given the special passport of courier to the Duke of Wellington to enable him to enter Verona freely past the guards (entry into Verona was blocked to all except official delegates). The Duke appears to have had a high regard for him: 'Allen anything you say must bear great weight with me.' [8] The Duke must have respected him as a man of great principle, even though he may have been puzzled at times by Allen's behaviour. When invited by the Duke to attend a dinner in order to meet some of the important people assembled for the Congress, he declined stating that he was only a humble individual and that he did not wish to come forward except where he had a duty to perform. This was not a very practical approach to the business in hand!

In 1822 Allen had three interviews with Emperor Alexander I – two in

Vienna and one in Verona after the Congress. As he commented in his diary of August 21st: 'My mind is, within this day or two pretty powerfully impressed with the feeling that it may possibly be right for me to meet the Emperor of Russia at Vienna.' [9] At the first Vienna meeting Allen presented the Emperor with letters from Wilberforce and Clarkson and urged the Emperor to take the lead at the forthcoming Congress in getting the Slave Trade banned as piracy. At the second interview the Emperor commented: 'When I am with you and such as you, I can breathe.' They knelt in prayer and then 'he embraced and kissed me.' [10] At the final interview they concluded the meeting by again praying together. Allen quotes the Emperor as saying: 'I not only respect you, but I love you from the bottom of my heart.' [11] This unusual friendship between a Quaker and visionary mystic lasted until the Emperor died in 1825.

The letter that Allen wrote to Prince Galitzin shortly after the Emperor's death is interesting: 'Never except in the loss of those most nearly connected with me by the ties of nature have I felt anguish of heart equal to that which I experienced when I first heard the news of the illness and death of the beloved Alexander. I am thankful that I yielded to the impression of duty which I felt in my own mind, to go to Vienna and confer with the dear Emperor.' [12]

Extract from a letter written by William Allen illustrating his use of the English ambassador's diplomatic bag for his letters.
(The Life of William Allen – Spitalfields Genius. Helena Hall.)

The range of Allen's interests abroad was huge: schools in Greece, land settlements in South Russia, missionary schools in Algeria, reform of Spanish prison conditions, Bavarian labourers colonies in South Germany and nearer home, education and land settlement in Ireland. Everywhere he made contacts – no wonder correspondence occupied so much of his time! So much correspondence followed his 1821 continental trip that ten of his friends joined together as a committee to assist with letters, circulation of books, Bibles, general advice and agricultural manuals. It is not clear how much was actually achieved following all this activity.

During his journeys abroad, Allen met many of the crowned heads of Europe, including the King of Bavaria and the King and Queen of Spain. At home, he became the lifelong friend and financial adviser of the Duke of Kent, fourth son of George III and father of Queen Victoria. Much later, Queen Victoria commented to Lord Bright that she was 'quite well informed about the Quakers. Mr. Allen was one of them and he was a great friend of my father's.' In 1831, Allen and Elizabeth Fry went to Kensington Palace to meet the Duchess of Kent and the young Princess Victoria. Following the marriage of the Queen to Prince Albert in 1840, Allen led the loyal address of the Quakers at Buckingham Palace.

Chapter 5
Marriages and Family Life

As Allen recorded in his diary in July 1796, he was 'disappointed in my expectations of a letter from my dear M.H. this morning ... very low today and oppressed with a variety of concerns.'[1] The reference was to Mary Hamilton who, overcoming her initial reluctance, married Allen at the Tottenham Quaker Meeting on November 13th 1796. Sadly, Mary died five days after the birth of her daughter, another Mary. Allen wrote in his diary of his 'tortured heart'.[2] The child was 'a sweet infant', but, thinking of 'how we should have enjoyed her together', he found it painful to nurse her. By 1804 he had obviously become devoted to his 'Precious jewel! I am almost afraid my affections are too strongly fixed upon her. Remember "He that loveth anything more than me, is not worthy of me" said the master himself.'[3]

Allen's religion and the distraction of hard work helped him to forget his sorrow at the death of his first wife. In January 1806 he married Charlotte Hanbury at the Devonshire House Meeting. This second marriage also ended sadly. When, in 1816, Allen, Charlotte, Elizabeth Fry and others made a missionary journey through Holland, Belgium and Germany and Switzerland, Charlotte was taken ill in Geneva and died.

In 1822 Allen's daughter married Cornelius Hanbury at Devonshire House Meeting in Bishopsgate. Over 800 guests attended, including Elizabeth Fry and Thomas Clarkson. Family history was to repeat itself when a year later Mary died in childbirth after the birth of her son William Allen Hanbury.

For years Allen and Grizell Birkbeck had been on friendly terms. According to the editors of his life and correspondence, 'The peculiar circumstances of his family led him often to seek her help and counsel; and in his close and deep bereavements, she was his kind, sympathising adviser.' Allen wrote a very significant letter to a friend in about March 1827: 'It was not, however, till after I lost my beloved child, who was, as it were, my last earthly prop, that a more intimate union than that of friendship opened to my view; and now the time nearly comes for its completion. We propose, if nothing unforeseen prevents, that the marriage shall take place on the 9th instant. Should this step appear singular, let it be remembered, that the dispensations through which I have had to pass, have been singularly afflictive.'[4]

The marriage took place on March 14th 1827, whereupon Allen took up residence at Grizell's house in Paradise Row, Stoke Newington.

Why did this marriage cause such consternation in Quaker circles, not only in London but also throughout the country? Allen, a minister of the Friends, was a public figure, internationally known for his anti-slavery views, his connections with the Royal Family especially with the Duke of Kent (whom he assisted with his financial affairs), and his meetings with the Emperor of Russia, for his social work and as a successful chemist with a flourishing London business. Grizell, at sixty-nine, was the wealthy widow of the banker Wilson Birkbeck. Allen was fifty seven. The authors of *Through a City Archway* suggest that Quakers did not generally approve of second, let alone third, marriages. However, remarriage after the death of a partner was quite common at that time. The Quaker Rules of Discipline in 1834 warned against overhasty marriages. This was hardly the case with Allen. Charlotte had died in 1816. David Hitchin, author of *Quakers in Lewes*, believes that 'the scandal as far as the Quakers were concerned related to unspoken concerns about age and sexuality while outsiders (who clearly didn't understand William Allen) thought first of financial gain.' The general disapproval, when the news of the proposed marriage became known, can be seen from the following letters: [5]

> 'Dear Joseph, The report about William Allen and Grizell Birkbeck intending to marry each other has been confirmed, but they did not pass the monthly meeting on the day first spoken of; the matter had been kept very private, and when it was divulged, it caused such a general sensation, or as a friend said in a letter, such an *Explosion*, and I believe general disapprobation, that the ardour of the Lovers seemed rather checked, and they let *that* monthly meeting pass over without publicly declaring their intentions. G.B. has several nieces (daughters of the late Thos. Bradshaw, who lived near Belfast), whom she has reared and educated from Children, I believe, and are like her own Daughters (having no child of her own). I understand they were much hurt when they heard of the matter, but that things have since been arranged to their satisfaction; the great agitation seems to have a good deal subsided, and I suppose the (not *young*) Couple will proceed at next monthly meeting – I have heard of two Women friends thrown ill in consequence of hearing of it. I apprehend, from what I consider pretty *good* authority, that the Bride elect is in the 70th year of her age – her Admirer is thought to be not more than in the 58th year of his age. I am thy affect. Brother. John Grubb.'

> 'If thou knew the torrent of disapprobation that W. Allen & G.B. intended Match has excited in this Country, probably thy astonishment might be even greater than it now is. When thou goes about to *defend* the matter, perhaps thou hadst better not bring G.F. & M.F.'

53

[George Fox & Margaret Fell] as an example of the propriety of this case, I believe the former, at the time of their marriage was about *45* years of age & the latter about *54* – very different from *56* and *70*, so the cases are not at all similar. It was not Susanna Corder or Elizabeth Dudley that were so deeply affected with this matter, but two married Women, Mothers of families, well acquainted with W.A. & G.B., and who wish well to the reputation of the Society & the consistency of its Members. We have seen a Copy of Verses written on the occasion, which has been printed in this new way called *Lithography* & circulated in various places. It is very severe, entitled *Friendly Scandal.* G.B. has a great property; it is said about £3000 a year.'

The report having reached the South of Ireland, Mary Watson wrote off at once to Grizell Birkbeck:

'Not believing the report respecting my much valued friends W.A. & G.B. I discouraged its circulation as derogatory to both, & forbore any expression to either of them on the subject, deeming it unnecessary – but contrary to my expectation and hope it appears now too much authenticated to leave room for doubt and it seems as though I could not rightly refrain from attempting to add my mite in that scale wherein I must believe much weight has already been thrown by the friends attached to both parties and to that precious Cause which I cannot doubt they have been called & qualified in their respective measures & stations to advocate. My dear friend G.B. long known and loved I have rejoiced in thy preservation & increasing dedication & usefulness.

Heartfelt would be my sorrow should any thing be permitted to obstruct that usefulness or obscure the brightness of that example which I believe has been productive of benefit to many. My highly esteemed friend W.A. stands in a still more awfully conspicuous point of view not only as minister in our own Society but the more public Theater *[sic]* of the world as an active promoter of religious & moral rectitude among man. Anything like a swerving from consistency in his steppings might extensively operate to retard that work, whereunto he was separated & has been made instrumental in promoting. It would afflict me, that from any cause the weight of his services should be lessened; in this land, where he has so recently & acceptably laboured, I am jealous lest it should be so, the rumour exciting general regret.

Suffer me then, my dear friends, to entreat your renewed close investigation of the subject in sincere desire that by the witnessing of that light, which is the true light, you may be enabled to discover the enemy if he has been permitted to approach you in this way to detect him in his transformations, resist him in his insinuations & become strengthened to turn from those things which though they may appear lawful, nevertheless may not be expedient for you. I cannot conceive, my dear friends, why you should not continue to enjoy the benefits & comforts of religious & social intercourse & fellowship as you have done for some years, independent, especially at thy time of life, of any view to a closer union. I have no objection to thy communicating the whole or any part of this to W.A. & hope by both it may be accepted as a proof of deep and sincere regard, & attachment wherein I remain thy affectionate friend, M.W.'

Grizell Birkbeck replied:

'Stoke Newington 2nd month 12th 1827.

My dear Friend, I have many times thought of taking up the pen to acknowledge thy kind letter, but have hardly felt strength to enter upon the subject, but we have for so many years known & loved each other, that I am not easy to pass it over in silence if it were only to tell thee that I accepted it as a token of thy affectionate solicitude on our account for which I am obliged. My dear Friend has entered so fully into our views and circumstances in reply to some kind letters sent us by our honourable & highly valued friend Sarah Grubb that I think I cannot do better than refer thee to that letter which thou mayest probably have already seen & if not, I have no doubt she will willingly communicate, and I may now add that after weighing the matter as well as we were able, we concluded it best to declare our intentions at our Monthly Meeting last fourth day, and with Gratitude & thankfulness to the Author of all Good I may acknowledge that I thought we had a favoured Meeting, in which my beloved cousin Anna Braithwaite was engaged in Solemn Supplication, John Shipley pretty largely in testimony, Sarah Harris shorter, all very acceptably, and I.S. paid a very satisfactory visit to our women's Meeting afterwards & my mind was clothed with precious calm & peaceful feelings, and however different the opinions of some of our friends may be from our own, the affectionate interest that many have evinced has been very gratifying, & I hope that nothing will diminish that love which I so highly value, & in the feeling of which I subscribe myself, thy affectionate Friend, Grizell Birkbeck. P.S. – Cousin William Allen desires his dear love to thyself, & thy daughter & my nieces, who are at home, request to unite with me in the same message.'

Grizell and William Allen appear to have lived happily together until her death in 1835. Two extracts from his diaries reveal something of Allen's feelings for her: 'Here was I comforted by a letter from my beloved wife; she is inexpressibly dear to me, and is indeed a true help meet.' On her death he wrote: 'How she was made a blessing to me in every way! Her judgment was sound, her integrity great; much as she loved me she always gave me up cheerfully for the service of the church ... Oh how I shall miss her society and love!' [6] The authors of *Through a City Archway* state that officially the Society of Friends never entirely exonerated Allen from blame for contracting a third marriage late in life to a rich woman, evidenced by the fact that in the formal 'Testimony concerning William Allen of the Gracechurch Monthly Meeting' issued soon after his death, the marriage was curtly dismissed in a brief sentence: 'In 1827 he was united in marriage to Grizell Birkbeck whom he survived.' [7] However, in a long testimony, understandably concerned mainly with Allen's achievements, only a few sentences are given to each of Allen's previous wives.

Family Life

It is difficult to glean much information about Allen's family life from his edited diaries, although he does speak of his distress at the death of his wives and his only daughter Mary: 'I had fondly looked to her, as to one calculated to be useful in the church and in the world at large and had hoped that she would be the comfort and support of my declining years, should they be lengthened out. But ah! It was otherwise ordered by Him who doeth all things well.' [8]

The best account of Allen's daily life comes from the memorials of Christine Majolier (later Alsop), the daughter of an old Quaker friend Louis Majolier. On his second continental journey Allen spent time with the Majoliers, and Christine, then a child of twelve, returned to England with Allen and his daughter Mary. She returned to France in 1820 but was back with the Allens in 1822. Christine's reminiscences give some insight into Allen's daily life at Plough Court and at Stoke Newington, the property that belonged to his second wife, Charlotte Hanbury. Mary Allen taught her. William Allen called her 'Criss', she called him father. She wrote: 'His life was one of continual engagements; he rose early, lighted his own fire and after his morning devotion, immediately began his correspondence. While he shaved, Mary read to him in Latin, usually from Livy. Directly after breakfast Anna Hanbury (Aunt Ann) used to read French to him: he seemed to have time for everything.' [9]

When Mary Allen married Cornelius Hanbury, 'Criss' was invited to come over again for a year to take charge of the family at Stoke Newington, for Anna Hanbury was in poor health. After Mary's death Criss took charge of her baby, William Allen Hanbury, and was 'mother' to him until he went to school in 1832. Many visitors came to the home at Stoke Newington, among them William Wilberforce, whom Christine describes as 'that active, slight man, who weighed only 76 lbs, including the 5 lbs for the iron stays he wore!'[10] William Allen used to bring the Plough Court business books to his home, where in fine weather they were carried to his summerhouse by his faithful servant 'Black Tom'. As Christine wrote: 'We used to spend the afternoon most pleasantly, he liked being read to while he was resting and much enjoyed having his grandson near him.'[11] In the summer of 1824 a German class was formed by William Allen, J. J. Lister, Edward Harris, Cornelius Hanbury, Lucy Bradshaw and Christine herself. Lessons were at seven in the morning and, according to Criss: 'With all that William Allen had upon him it was astonishing how earnest he was, and how industriously he laboured. He entered into all that related to improvement in teaching, and he was very sanguine in everything he undertook.'[12]

Directly after breakfast Allen went regularly to town (to Plough Court to attend meetings). He returned for a three o'clock dinner, often bringing company with him. His foreign correspondence was very large and he spent time in his study most days. Christine acted as Allen's French correspondent, but he always copied any letters himself and he was efficient in using oiled and black paper to produce two copies at a time. 'He was very neat in all he did; he seemed literally to have time for everything. The evening would be filled up with experiments, observation of the stars, the posting* of the business books and the countless 'odd jobs' which filled up every spare minute.'[13]

Christine includes a description of life at Gravelye, the cottage which Allen occupied when he stayed in Lindfield. His house was, she states, ever open to receive 'all the strangers who required his aid and protection. Men of all countries, Russians, Germans, Frenchmen, Swedes, Greeks, Italians, Spaniards, North American Indians, West Indians and many of the suffering sons of West Africa partaking of that hospitality which he knew so well how to bestow without the least ostentation, very little difference being made between their entertainment and the dinners given to Lord Brougham, Dr. Lushington, Wilberforce, John Smith, of Dale Park, or distinguished foreigners. Many a stranger in a strange land has indeed found in him a true friend.'[14]

After the death of Grizell in 1835, two of her nieces, Lucy and Elizabeth Bradshaw, looked after him. By 1839 his health was failing: 'I have

---

* entering business transactions in a ledger.

certainly been much overdone and am too anxious; I must make a change; my memory is failing.' Fayle has this to say: 'Busy to the last, now writing for the Lindfield Register, now exposing the tyranny of the Ecclesiastical Courts, in which the Quaker, William Baines, for a demand of £2 5s. had to pay £127 8s., as costs. Again, helping in the formation of the Pharmaceutical Society of Chemists and Druggists (April 4th, 1841), writing to the King of Sweden on behalf of the persecuted little flock of "Friends" under his sway; visiting Gravelye by the "Brighton railroad, opened on the 12th (July 1841), to Haywards Heath"; entertaining Lord Brougham, – a "very satisfactory visit", for it was about education and presenting an address to the King of Prussia on behalf of the little Quaker community at Minden.' Amidst all this activity, Fayle added that, in his final years, Allen felt comfort 'in having such a quiet retreat as Lindfield.'[15]

Already, some twenty five years before, he had written of quite serious heart trouble and of the need 'to take double care not to overload myself with engagements.' Even so, in 1840 he spent five months on the continent, travelling about 5000 miles.

Christine describes her last meeting with him: 'A committee had been appointed to visit Friends in the south of France; and I left London, via Southampton, in company with them, on the 20th of the Eight Month, 1840. Peter Bedford, George Stacey, Josiah Forster, Samuel Fox, and Thomas Norton, Jun., formed our party; and at Southampton we met William Allen and Lucy Bradshaw, who were to accompany us as far as Paris. Thus I had the pleasure of a little more of dear William Allen's company. Before he left the hotel in Paris, he told me that he wished to give me a trifle to get something in remembrance of him. I felt that we were parting probably for the last time. My heart was too full for utterance. He was affected too. It was indeed the last time that I saw this beloved friend, who had for so many years been like a father to me.'[16] Allen wrote from Lindfield in early summer 1843: 'I endeavour to divide my time between this place and Stoke Newington being affectionately cared for by my niece Lucy Bradshaw.' As he wrote to Susanna Corder: 'I believe this illness is sent in mercy to me. To wean me more and more from all things below and to make me look more steadily to the end of time.'[17] After an eleven-week illness he died on December 30th 1843, aged 73 years. He was buried in the Quaker burial ground at Stoke Newington.

Chapter 6
Political and Personal Satire and Brief Description of 1827 Caricatures

The late eighteenth and early nineteenth centuries saw a rapid growth of newspapers and journals. By the end of the eighteenth century there were twelve London papers and sixty provincial ones. With the improvement of roads news could be transported more quickly. Newspapers were often shared and read in coffee houses, taverns and inns. There was a love of gossip and scandal, especially if it related to the rich and powerful. Shop windows were filled with coloured cartoons, which were fiercely political or libellously personal. The lampoons on the Royal Family, especially the Prince Regent, later George IV, are good examples.

During the course of the eighteenth century the caricature was transformed from an exclusive dilettante amusement into a powerful form of social and political critique. William Hogarth had a relatively select sale, but towards the end of the eighteenth century there was a proliferation of amateur prints and a broadening scope of graphic satire. The regular works of Thomas Rowlandson, James Gillray and his successor George Cruikshank dominated the 'golden age of caricature'. In the early nineteenth century there was a slow demise in this type of caricature. Diana Donald discusses the changes in *The Age of Caricature*: 'The work of reformers encouraged a more serious attitude; the view developed that satire should be a good-humoured corrective of folly in society at large, not just savage and vulgar. By the late 1820s the lithographs of John Doyle – naturalistic portraits of politicians, which were only mildly satirical, superseded the envenomed caricatures of the revolutionary period. The Queen's affair[1] in 1820 provoked the last great upsurge of lewd and insulting caricatures in the eighteenth century tradition. Novels, annuals and magazines were being purchased for respectable family reading.'[2]

The seven 1827 caricatures relating to Allen's third marriage are less extreme in *style* than they might have been, but not in content. According to Diana Donald: 'The cynicism about supposedly mercenary marriages with older women was a humorous commonplace throughout the Georgian period as was the tendency to attack groups like the Quakers and the Methodists for supposed moral humbug.' However, an attack of this kind as late as 1827 was surprising. By that time figures in public life were generally treated with a bit more respect. Did Allen have personal enemies who may have incited the print publishers?[3] He had difficulties in his dealings with Robert Owen and Joseph Lancaster, but neither seems likely to have acted in this way. Was the marriage the subject of comment in the national press? In view of Allen's position in public life and the open disapproval of Quakers, comment in the press was very likely. It is interesting that M. Dorothy George states that the caricatures against the marriage are allegedly from a Quaker source. The intended match would have been seen as evidence of basic weakness and consequent corruption of moral values: 'The zest for scandal was unabated, despite, or because of, the stirrings of what it is convenient to call Victorianism.' [4] If the Quakers were in disarray and discomforted, then the lampoonists would enjoy a field day.

The caricatures took full advantage of the fact that Grizell was known to be wealthy. How did Allen react to the unpleasant publicity? He may well have found the prints very wounding. He had a prosperous business and was a man of simple tastes not likely to require additional financial resources – unless it was to further his social work. Diana Donald's opinion is that people seldom commented in public when pilloried in this way, as that often provoked further ridicule. William Wilberforce made it a rule not to respond to public or personal attacks. He was later to grieve that he had not defended his character sufficiently!

Brief Description of the Caricatures

The Modern Alchymist – coloured etching by T. Jones, published March 8th, 1827. [See reproduction on page 81.]

Allen is in Quaker dress and riding boots. Behind Allen are crucibles containing the personifications of various concepts from which captions emerge. The main central crucible labelled 'matter of money' contains the witch-like head of Mrs Birkbeck. Gold coins pour out of her mouth into a tub! The implication is that all Allen's professed beliefs and support for good causes are pious humbug now that he has discovered 'the goose that layeth the golden eggs'.

Sweet William and Grizzell or Newington Nunnery in an Uproar – Robert Cruikshank, March 5th, 1827. [Illustration courtesy of Sue Blunden.] (See also another version reproduced in colour on page 84.)

This cartoon is set in a Friends' Meeting House. Allen stands facing Grizell. She asks: 'Is there no hope for me Dear William?' He suggests that she read Genesis 21, which relates how Abraham (100 years old) and Sarah (90 years old) had a son Isaac. Cupid may not have as much power as formerly but 'all so say Love never can diminish or grow cold.' The words then mock the relationship: 'She doats upon the very man. He doats upon her Gold.' The second version of the same print (see page 84) adds the words: 'To be sure the Beef is rather old, But then the Grizzles made of gold.'

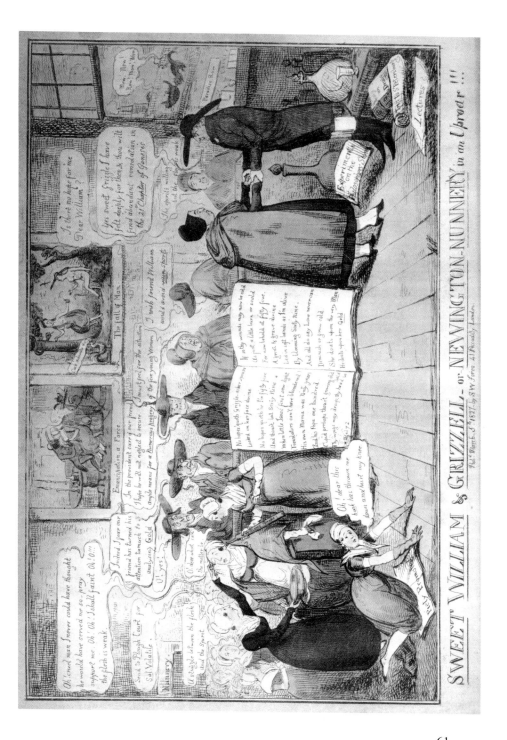

There are two pictures on the wall. The first shows a black man (a mocking reference to Allen's apparent high ideal of emancipation) kissing a white lady bearing a strong resemblance to Grizell. The ignored boiling kettle suggests the traditional sanctity of hearth and home is being overlooked. The other picture shows Allen and Grizell as Adam and Eve in 'The Fall of Man' where a rooster cries 'Cock a doodle doo'.

The group of young women on the left side of the caricature may include Grizell's nieces, Lucy, Anna and Eliza Bradshaw who often stayed with her. Their unmarried status may have given rise to the title Newington Nunnery, but there is also an even stronger connection with the Quaker Boarding School in Stoke Newington run by Susanna Corder. The lady in a faint with the words, 'Oh cruel man I could never have thought he would have served me so ...', is Susanna (as checked with a likeness of her in the library of the Religious Society of Friends in Britain), and she is referred to as the governess by one of the girls in the background of the print. The helper who says, 'Send to Plough Court for Sal Volatile', is making a reference of course to Allen's business. There is yet another mocking reference to the corruption of moral ideals with the scene of a girl who has stumbled on a book written on the subject of piety. In the background there is a group of strongly disapproving Quaker men and women with again an allusion to money: 'Our friend has turned his attention too much to analysing Gold.' There is a reference to: 'I must feel for the situation of the five young women.' Grizell had five nieces living with her when she married Allen – *probably the five young girls nearest to Susanna*. It would be easy to adopt a modern slant on this statement. Allen is known to have enjoyed the company of ladies and made references to his 'dear nieces'. It is not known how they felt about this marriage but they may well have 'wept' for the loss of financial expectations. Their aunt's wealth, under contemporary law, would have become her husband's on marriage. Since she was too old to have children, it would pass to his heirs. However, any suggestion of impropriety would be totally wrong – the concern was with the loss of a good example of high moral standards.

Willy the Lion Insulted by Asses – G. Williams, 1827.
[The Library of the Religious Society of Friends in Britain.]

Mrs Birkbeck, in Quaker dress, holds a ribbon which goes round the neck of the lion which represents Allen – recognisable by the face and hat. The word 'union' on the ribbon is a reference to the forthcoming marriage. Both turn their heads in profile towards two asses. The asses have Quaker heads and are laughing and jeering. This caricature is reminiscent of Aesop's fables – in fact it is described as a fable illustrated. 'Jeer on and be asses still', says the lion. The moral is that it is below the dignity of a great

mind to entertain contests with people that have neither quality nor courage. This caricature, which is unusual as it is sympathetic to Allen and Grizell Birkbeck, could have been promoted by friends.

Yea! Verily the Spirit moveth or the Wedding day of William and Grizell – March 1827. [The Library of the Religious Society of Friends in Britain.]

Again the references to the Old Testament and to Allen doating on her gold. The reference to Grizell burying two husbands already is incorrect. She was married only once before. The pious Quaker on the right makes a reference to Plough Court pharmacy and to Grizell's age. He says: 'Plough up the Fallow Ground Friend, perchance it may be fruitful.' There is the same row of disapproving Quakers in the background.

Untitled Caricature.
[The Library of the Religious Society of Friends in Britain.]

The message of the empty cradle and disappointed females is clear enough – but there are no slanderous or vicious words attached to the picture.

Racing Intelligence or Money makes the mare to go – published March 8th, 1827 by R. Cruikshank. [See reproduction on page 81.]

In this caricature Allen and Mrs Birkbeck are seen in a race with Allen in the lead. They have almost reached a Friends Meeting House. Signpost points back 'To Wisdom' (reversed lettering). The heat has caused great speculation. The winner, who is expected to be Alchemist (Allen), will pocket many thousands from the day's sports. There is a reference in the

script to his earlier marriages (the maiden plate against Hamiltonian out of Mary) and (the Tottenham purse against Capel). Allen's first marriage was to Mary Hamilton and his second to Charlotte Hanbury. Capel was a commonly used Christian name in the Hanbury family. Plate referred to the gold or silver cup once the prize in a horse race.

The Attraction of Gravity – an unrecorded caricature – by an unidentified artist, March 1827. [The Wellcome Library, London.]

The drawing shows Allen and Grizell in Quaker dress. The Plough is a reference to Allen's business as are the words 'receiver' and 'retort'. 'Animadvert' means to pass censure on conduct. The meaning of the words below the caricature is obscure.

Chapter 7
Contemporary Educational Views

At the beginning of the eighteenth century the Society for the Promoting of Christian Knowledge had made big efforts to establish charity schools. 'Children are made tractable and submissive by being early accustomed to Awe and Punishment and Dutiful Subjection. From such timely Discipline the Publick may expect Honest and Industrious Servants.'[1] However, by the end of the eighteenth century the provision of schools for the poor was still very limited. Some of the old free grammar schools had fallen into decay, charity schools were not easy to establish without the financial backing of the classes who questioned their necessity, and the poor themselves often felt the need to put their children out to work at an early age to assist the family income. Interestingly, there was also some distrust of provided education, and dame schools (maligned by educational reformers) were sometimes preferred. Some dame schools did provide a little basic education. Reading could be obtained for 1d or 2d a week. Writing as well would be 3d or 4d a week.

The main obstacle to the development of schools for the poor was the attitude of the richer classes, summed up in the words of Bishop Dampier in 1793: 'The Happiness and Virtue of the poor man consists in studying to be quiet and to mind his own business.' The poor should accept the status quo – education might lead to the questioning of the poor's allotted place in society. (These views were reinforced by events in Revolutionary France, for recent memories inevitably struck fear in to the hearts of men of property.) The motive behind the Sunday School Movement (spread by such men as John Pounds and Robert Raikes) was to keep poor children off the streets and out of mischief. Instruction was confined to teaching the catechism and knowledge of the Bible. As the time available was limited, little more than reading was attempted. Writing was regarded as an unnecessary skill and an inappropriate activity for a Sunday. Teachers were generally volunteers, so education was inexpensive. An attempt was made to instil virtues of thrift, obedience and industry. By 1813 it was calculated that 452,000 children in England and Wales attended Sunday schools, 168,000 went to Church schools and 53,000 to dame schools. This still left many gaps, but in the early nineteenth century any idea that the State should provide education was unacceptable to the majority of people. State intervention could lead to a reduction in individual liberty. A tradition had developed that charities financed and ran schools, hospitals and almshouses.

William Allen was certainly not alone in his belief that the poor should be educated. Philanthropists of all religious opinions increasingly adopted the cause. Rapid urbanisation and the great increase in population in the late eighteenth century led to social problems – poverty, vagrancy and delinquency. More efficient printing and cheaper production of paper meant that newspapers, pamphlets, tracts and books became more available and there was a growing desire amongst the poor themselves to learn to read. As early as 1798 Malthus declared that it was 'a national disgrace' that the education of the lower classes was left to a few Sunday schools – many which had started by teaching arithmetic and writing now restricted the curriculum to reading.

Attitudes towards elementary education within the Church of England

Although many were largely indifferent, philanthropists (and shrewd tacticians?) began to appreciate the need for change. J. Taylor quotes Samuel Horsley's Charity School address in 1793 in which he referred to the 'capricious domination of an unprincipled rabble in France' [2], but concluded that it would be more dangerous to exclude the poor from religious education than to leave them in ignorance. A limited education would teach children disciplined habits beneficial to employers – the virtues of thrift, obedience and acceptance of one's lot in life could be emphasised. In the 1790s increasing numbers of bishops gave support to the Sunday and Charity School Movements.

Suspicion arose about the work of the Dissenters Joseph Lancaster, Allen and his friends and their campaign for universal non-denominational education. True, Allen argued that 'this would lessen those prejudices and animosities which often have been found so mischievous in society'; and a number of politicians such as Holland, Whitbread and Brougham, radical philosophers such as Bentham, some Evangelical churchmen, and supporters of the working man – Francis Place and Robert Owen – supported the campaign. However, the Anglican Church became fearful of losing its privileged position as the established church, since that carried with it the opportunity of influencing the religious and social attitudes of the young. Indeed, Mrs Sarah Trimmer led a spirited verbal campaign in its support. She had been responsible for organising a School of Industry for Orphans in Bradford in 1787. She also established a Sunday school to teach children to read the Scriptures and to instil knowledge of Christian duties and correct conduct for their station in life. She advocated the founding of a School of Industry in every parish. Poor girls were to be instructed how to spin and learn needlework of the useful kind and how to knit stockings. Small rewards for good work should be given. Parents should accustom them to wash, iron and mend their clothes but their education should not be left to 'their ignorant and corrupt parents'. She published a book *The Oeconomy of Charity*, outlining her views. She was alarmed when, in 1805, George III not only received Joseph Lancaster but also became an annual subscriber to his school. A fear of disturbing the status quo had led to inaction by the Church of England. Sarah Trimmer argued that if Joseph Lancaster's non-denominational schools became widely accepted then the influence of the Church of England would be undermined. In her book *The Guardian of Education* Sarah Trimmer accused Lancaster of stealing his ideas on the monitorial system from Dr Bell who had used similar methods when out in Madras. The Anglican Society founded in 1811 aimed to establish schools where religious teaching would be based on the tenets of the Church of England. It developed into the National School Society. The British and Foreign School Society was founded in 1814. The battle lines were drawn. Rivalry and sectarianism were to dog developing state education throughout the nineteenth century and beyond.

Hannah More's work in Somerset

It is interesting to compare the Anglican Hannah More's work in Somerset with that of William Allen in Lindfield. Both philanthropists believed in the need to educate the poor, arguing that if they were taught to read the Bible they would automatically acquire an understanding of what was right or wrong. In 1789 William Wilberforce visited Cheddar. Afterwards he wrote to Hannah More: 'Miss Hannah More something must be done for Cheddar. If you will be at the trouble, I will be at the expense.' [3] Hannah More was to be influential in the setting up of schools in Cheddar, Shipham and Axbridge, in spite of meeting with strong opposition from the gentry, local farmers and the Church. Landlords and farmers were anxious about their supply of cheap casual labour. Fears were strong that the education of the poor would encourage subversive political activities. Hannah had a long battle with the Bishop of Bath and Wells. 'My object is not to make fanatics but to train up the lower classes in habits of industry and piety.' Hannah More's task was not easy. Shipham and its immediate neighbour Rowberrow were described as 'two depraved and wretched mining villages at the top of the Mendips – the people savage and brutal in their natures and ferocious in their manners.' [4] No constable would ever venture to arrest a Shipman man!

The Sunday and weekday school, opened for Shipham and Rowberrow in 1790, provide an example of her work. Pupils were taught to read passages from the Scriptures, but writing was thought to be an unnecessary accomplishment which might 'give them ideas'. Some refused to send their children unless they received a payment; others suspected that the whole scheme was a plot to kidnap children and sell them as slaves. The girls were taught to sew, knit and spin, and given general training for work as domestics. Boys were given some sort of industrial work. Bibles and Prayer Books were presented as rewards. In addition gingerbread was a useful bribe once in six weeks. Clothing was given out once a year. Hannah More worked hard to establish her week-day schools of Industry – a visit to which meant a 30 mile circuit on horseback. On her death in 1833 the schools were dissolved, but her work illustrates that in different parts of the country the educational needs of the poor were being addressed.

Chapter 8

Allen's Involvement with Lancaster, Owen, and the Fleetwood House School

William Allen's relationship with Joseph Lancaster and the development of the British and Foreign School Society (BFSS)

Allen's diaries, the minutes of the Lancasterian Society, BFSS and correspondence reveal the significant part played by Allen in Joseph Lancaster's affairs and the events leading to the formation of the BFSS. Allen must have read Quaker Joseph Lancaster's book entitled *Improvements in Education as it effects the Labouring Classes of the Community* (1803). Lancaster appealed directly to George III: 'Many thousands of thy subjects have no proper knowledge of their duty to thee, nor to the community at large for want of proper education and knowledge of the Scriptures.' The King responded: 'It is my wish that every poor child in my kingdom may be taught to read the Bible.' In addition, the teaching of a trade would assist industry and independence. The education of the lower classes, especially in London, was becoming an important issue in Whig and radical circles. Lancaster's Borough Road School, Southwark, established about 1798, quickly gained important subscribers including the King himself and other members of the Royal Family.

In 1808 Allen visited Lancaster's Borough Road School and was much impressed: 'I can never forget the impression the scene made upon me. Here I beheld a 1000 children collected from the streets where they were learning nothing but mischief – one bad boy corrupting another all reduced to the most perfect order and training to subordination and usefulness and learning the great truths of the Gospels from the Bible.'[1] Like Lancaster, Allen believed that the monitorial system was a cheap and efficient method of educating large numbers of poor children. An older child received instruction from the master and in turn endeavoured to instruct his group. With strict discipline enforced one master could effectively manage 500 even 1000 pupils at a yearly expense for each child of 5 to 6 shillings. (Compare the expense with Allen's one shilling and two pence boyhood telescope!) A year later he wrote: 'The more I consider the subject of general education, the more I am convinced of its importance; the poor will be brought to a knowledge of their duty, which is one step toward the diminution of crime and as the physical strength of the community resides in this class, it is of the utmost importance that the individuals composing it

*Joseph Lancaster,
from an engraving by Dequevauller, from Vigneron's lithograph c.1918.
(Library of the Religious Society of Friends in Britain.)*

should have clear ideas of right or wrong.'[2] Such sentiments help to explain why members of the Royal Family, Whig aristocrats, middle class merchants and bankers gave financial support to Lancaster. Juvenile delinquency in London was high. Unemployment in areas such as Spitalfields aggravated social problems. When local Quakers opened one of the earliest London Lancasterian Schools in Spicer Street Spitalfields, Allen supported the venture. His support for Lancaster was not unqualified, however. As he observed after meeting him in 1808: '[Lancaster was] possessed of a very great and beneficial idea, his intentions were honourable, but he had great faults and needed careful management,'[3] a criticism that was justified. Although Lancaster possessed talent for educating children, he was totally unable to manage his financial affairs. In 1808, with debts of £600 sterling, he was in danger of imprisonment by creditors and was rescued only because Joseph Fox advanced him £200. Allen appreciated the danger to the whole Lancasterian School Plan: 'The whole thing would be irretrievably ruined if he (Lancaster) had sole management of it.' Allen proposed that Lancaster appoint a Committee of six to meet regularly. He himself offered to encourage as many Friends as possible to support the venture. At first Lancaster opposed, fearing he would lose control, but he eventually agreed. Many of the committee, including Allen, offered private assistance to Lancaster until loans could be raised and annual subscriptions increased. As a Committee member and then Treasurer, Allen was to play a significant role in putting finances on a secure footing.

The difficulties with Lancaster did not end there, however. Surviving correspondence of Allen's from 1816 describes Lancaster's anger when the committee would not keep a carriage for him. Lancaster refused to keep accounts and proceeded to take an expensive place at Tooting without consultation. He acquired a chariot and four-wheeled chaise and ran up debts for hired horses. Lancaster, it seemed to Allen, was 'intoxicated with the applause he had received' and slighted all advice.[4] The solution of the committee was to take over the Borough Road School, and change the name of the movement to the British and Foreign School Society (BFSS). The newly formed organisation went from strength to strength, training increasing numbers of masters and mistresses and setting up nonconformist schools in other parts of Britain and throughout the world. Insufficient credit has been given to Allen for the part he played in the development of the BFSS. School meetings, canvassing for money, journeys and correspondence all absorbed much time, as diary entries reveal:

> 1811 – 'Very much overdone this week. I think school concerns altogether have taken up nearly three days.'[5]

1812 – 'Of all the concerns that I have anything to do with, the Lancasterian lies the most heavily on my mind.'[6]

1814 – 'Busy at school accounts, much exhausted.'[7]

Lancaster did not take criticism kindly. In 1816 he published a book, 'Oppression and Persecution', in which he openly attacked Fox and Allen. As Allen wrote to a friend: 'As Joseph Lancaster has abused me in print it may be enough to state that I have been principally restrained from exposing him from tenderness to a Man, who, bad as he is, has been highly useful and because I know that the Enemies of the Good cause would triumph in such exposure'[8] (a reference to the National Society and its Anglican membership).

Allen was in full support of the BFSS view, both on religious and financial grounds, that religious education should be non-denominational. The majority of BFSS members were Quakers or members of other nonconformist sects. Without government support strong financial backing from members was essential, and belief and practical needs went together.

The strong conviction of both Joseph Fox and William Allen that the Bible was to be the sole reading book used in the Society's schools led inevitably to dispute. Francis Place, the radical politician, for a short time a committee member of the Society, described Fox as a 'gloomy bigot'. Allen, he wrote later in his autobiography, was 'too credulous and too affectionate and too compassionate to his friend to suspect he was imposed upon.'[9] Allen's views on the use of the Bible alone were in fact as inflexible as those of Fox. Allen was in a difficult position. He endeavoured to retain links with those interested in more secular education such as Place and Jeremy Bentham. When Place showed Allen three illustrated reading lessons, Allen stated that he was very much pleased with the plan of the Picture Book: 'I am sure that the idea may be used to very good purpose.' However, the withdrawal of Place from the committees of the BFSS and the West London Lancasterian Association appears to have eased the situation. In 1820, an English version of scripture lessons based on extracts from the Bible, drawn up by Quakers for use in Russian monitorial schools and with an introduction by Allen, was introduced into all BFSS schools. This remained the only permitted reading material until 1839 when the use of secular reading books was allowed.[6]

As a member of the African Institution Allen also played a prominent role. Several reviews in *The Philanthropist* (the journal he produced with Mill) dealt with Negro welfare and education both in Sierra Leone and in the West Indies. Young Negroes were sent to Borough Road to 'learn the system' before returning home to set up schools. Allen recorded in his diary in 1814 that on the day before they left England he 'had all the African boys to tea.' Bartle notes that a foreign fund was set up by Allen and special subscriptions raised to pay the expenses of teachers sent abroad, but inevitably funds were not sufficient for the mammoth task ahead. However, in 1829 the BFSS debt was at last paid off: 'Thus has Divine Providence been pleased to crown this most interesting work with success,' Allen wrote in his diary.[10] The improved financial position meant that a full time secretary, Henry Dunn, could be appointed. Treasury building grants were successfully negotiated and the number of BFSS schools in the Midlands and the North was increased.

Although Allen continued to attend committee meetings and manage the society's finances as treasurer, he began to play a less active role in the BFSS as the Lindfield plans began henceforth to account for much of his time and money.

William Allen's Relationship with Robert Owen

Allen was undoubtedly influenced by Robert Owen, even though he was also to disagree fiercely with him. In 1813 Robert Owen published *A New View of Society*. Orthodox thinking was that the poor were poor because they were idle, vicious, intemperate and ignorant. Poverty, therefore, was a just consequence of their sins. Owen's radical view was that 'Man's character is made for and not by him.' Education and environment were all important. If the poor were lifted out of their poverty and were better fed, clothed and housed and given educational opportunities their character would be transformed. At New Lanark Owen endeavoured to create a model community. Houses provided for workers were enlarged, sanitation improved, working hours shortened, and the shops were to provide cheap and good quality food and clothes.

In 1814 articles of partnership were signed by Allen, Bentham, Owen and four other partners to buy the New Lanark Mills to carry out Owen's scheme for social amelioration. The terms included a clause that all children on the estate were to be educated on the British or other approved system. Definite religious instruction should be given. The authorised version of the Bible was to be the only book used. From the beginning, however, Allen appears to have had doubts about Owen and his peculiar opinions, as shown by a diary statement of October 30th 1815: 'Much depressed from various causes, I am uneasy about Lanark and have written a long letter to Robert Owen. It is now the general opinion that my friend is the determined enemy of all revealed religion .... We came into the concern not to form a manufactory of infidels but to support a benevolent character in plans of a very different nature, in which the happiness of millions *[sic]* and the cause of morality and virtue are deeply concerned.'[11]

*Robert Owen by William Henry Brooke.
(By courtesy of the National Portrait Gallery, London.)*

In 1816 Owen expounded his views before a Select Committee of the House of Commons, set up to inquire into the education of the 'lower orders'. Owen testified that he had adopted 'a combination of the Madras (Bell) and the British and Foreign System with other parts that experience had pointed out.' Education was for the formation of character – correct and loving attitudes to each other and to society were more important than the mere mechanics of learning. Children should not be annoyed with books, which should not be introduced until the age of ten. Curiosity should lead them to ask questions. The classroom for younger pupils at his Institution for the Formation of Character was hung with specimens of minerals and representations of animal life. The curriculum consisted of Natural History, Geography, History, Reading, Writing and Arithmetic and Sewing for the girls. With older children rewards and punishments were barred. There was great emphasis on teaching the little ones dancing, singing and military exercises. Owen's views on the purpose of Sunday were clearly expressed. Sunday to Owen was a day for enjoyment and exercise instead of 'one of superstitious gloom and tyranny over the mind.' Such views were in sharp contrast to those held by Allen and his Quaker partners. The dancing might make a good show for visitors, but it was too worldly, and the military exercises were an affront to their pacifist convictions. Apparently Allen also objected to the Roman tunics worn by both boys and girls and he was anxious to get the boys into pantaloons! Owen was too much of a materialist for Allen and he increasingly wished to dissociate himself from Owen's secular environmentalism. There seemed to be too much concern with the good of the body rather than the salvation of the soul!

For Allen, the Quaker partners' visit to New Lanark in 1818 was 'a trying week, as I have had deep exercise of mind on account of Robert Owen's infidel principles. I have sustained many disputes with him. What I pray for is to be favoured to see clearly what is required for me to do. Oh! That He whom I wish to love and to serve, would favour me with light and clearness.'[12] The partners even took the step of asking a local minister to visit Owen's school to check what was being taught and to correspond with them if he saw any attempt to introduce anything contrary to revealed religion!

With the backing of the London partners, Allen wrote to Owen about his concerns, but Owen appears to have ignored Allen's complaints. In 1822 a diary entry noted: 'I have made up my mind to have no more discussions with Robert Owen about his principles that being clearly a waste of time.'[13] In 1824, after a further visit by Foster and Allen to New Lanark, they succeeded in obtaining an agreement by virtue of which some Bible instruction was to be given in the schools, and singing, apart from psalms, drawing and teaching of musical instruments were no longer to be supplied by the committee. A well-trained master from the Borough Road School was to ensure that proper instruction was given. There was also to be a public reading of the Holy Scriptures each week, as well as evening lectures on Chemistry and Natural History, which the local population could attend. Allen noted: 'My mind was much relieved. I believe that through the whole of this deeply trying and exercising business Divine support has been near.'[14] The rift remained. Owen withdrew from the management of New Lanark Mills and gave up his partnership in 1829. Allen retained his financial interest until 1835.

In the autobiography he wrote years later, Owen described Allen as 'a man of great pretensions in his sect, a very busy, bustling, meddling character, making great professions of friendship to me, yet underhandedly doing all in his power to undermine my views and authority.'[15] He added in a later passage: 'William Allen returned from the continent of Europe where he had come personally into communication with the Emperor Alexander of Russia and with some other crowned heads, which turned his head into a wrong channel for usefulness. His mind was linked to Quaker prejudices and the Lancasterian system of defective education, which I had materially assisted to make what it was, but the limited and religious prejudices of Lancaster's committee would not allow it to proceed further and William Allen in particular thought this small step the perfection of education. [Owen means 'the achievements' to date – Lancaster's monitorial system and non-denominational religious instruction with the Bible as the sole reading material.] On his return he worked to depreciate all my proceedings because I had denounced publicly all the superstitions and false religions of the world ... He recommended the abandonment of my mode ... for his petty Quaker notions and his supposed superior benefits to be derived from religion ... without music, dancing or military discipline, all so essential to form a good and superior rational character.'[16] Even so, Owen admitted that Allen was 'most desirous of doing good in his own way.'[17] In the case of Joseph Lancaster it was a matter of a volatile reckless personality at odds with a committee determined to save the Plan; and whereas Owen, whose views, like Pestalozzi's, were in advance of his time, is now rightly seen as one of the great educational innovators, Allen was influenced entirely by his religious beliefs.

The Fleetwood House Boarding School

In 1824 Allen, Grizell Birkbeck, Anna Hanbury and Susanna Corder were among the Quaker proprietors who opened a girls boarding school for the children of Friends in Stoke Newington. The fees were fifty pounds a year, washing not included. The girls wore plain Quaker dresses and bonnets, much to the amusement of the pupils of another girls' school nearby. There was a wide curriculum – English, Writing, Arithmetic, Geography, Astronomy and the use of the Globes, History, Physics, Chemistry, Experimental Philosophy, Natural History, French and Needlework. The Head Mistress was a Quaker minister, Susanna Corder. Allen offered his assistance as a chemistry teacher.[18] He took a keen interest in the school's progress and noted in his Journal for 16th January 1826: 'The Friends' girls' school at Newington, under the care of Susanna Corder, prospers. I generally attend the readings there on first and fourth-day readings, and they are often times of spiritual refreshment.'[19] He sometimes took his telescope so that the pupils could view the stars. Before her marriage, a Mrs Sophia de Morgan sometimes attended Allen's chemistry lectures and she made some interesting comments: '... made the acquaintance of William Allen, who kindly allowed me to attend the lectures on chemistry which he gave, with experiments, to a class of young girls ... Mr Allen's quick perception of facts was greater than his power of following out extensive inferences. He was a good observer and classifier, but stopped at facts and phenomena. In philanthropy the same ready perception and hastiness of inference were apparent. His exceeding benevolence and strong impulse to help the suffering led him occasionally into exaggeration of the evils he opposed; but all good causes need pioneers who overdo their work at first. Without such the work would not be done.'[20]

Taken from the print by R. Burgess, Portraits of doctors and scientists in the Wellcome Institute, 1973, no.55.4. (The Wellcome Library, London.)

(Museum of the Royal Pharmaceutical Society of Great Britain.)

John Bellers, panel E2. Quaker Tapestry Scheme ©

Elizabeth Fry and the patchwork quilts, panel E6. Quaker Tapestry Scheme ©

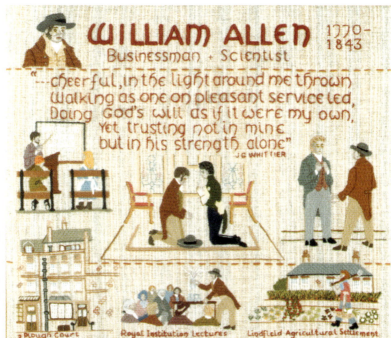

William Allen, Panel E12. Quaker Tapestry Scheme ©

The Slave Trade, Panel F3. Quaker Tapestry Scheme ©

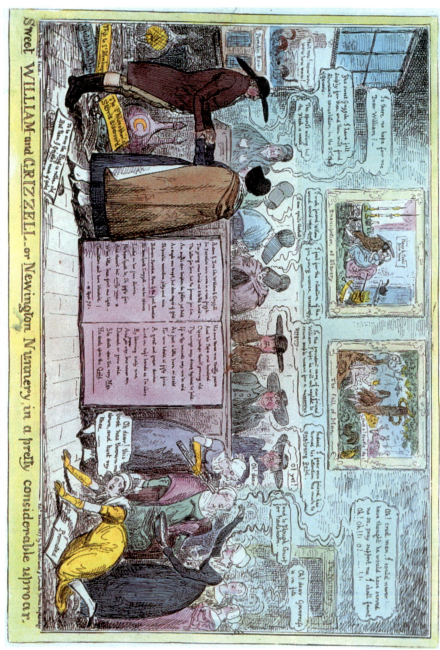

(Library of the Religious Society of Friends in Britain.)

Chapter 9
Rural Communities – Social and Economic Conditions

Significant changes in agriculture took place from the mid eighteenth century to the early nineteenth century. The introduction of vaccination against smallpox and a greater understanding of the importance of cleanliness led to a steep rise in population. The population growth boosted the demand for food. High prices due to wartime inflation served to encourage investment in agriculture as profits rose. The old system, in which open fields of land were divided into strips and worked by the majority of villagers, was replaced by a more productive system of farming. New enclosed farms led to the widespread adoption of more scientific farming, increased crop rotation, drainage and the beginning of machinery.

The enclosure of agricultural and common land drove many yeomen farmers, cottagers and smallholders into service as landless agricultural labourers. They could not afford the cost of hedging and ditching or the loss of grazing rights on common land, which the enclosure movement involved. In his Rural Rides William Cobbett lamented the disappearance of the yeoman farmer. 'A labouring man in England, with a wife and only three children, though he never loses a day's work, though he and his family be economical, frugal and industrious, is not now able to procure for himself by his labour, a single meal of meat from one end of the year to the other. Is this a state in which the labouring man ought to be?' By 1790 about three-quarters of all agricultural land was being cultivated by tenants. Cobbett warned: 'When farmers become gentlemen, their labourers become slaves.' As well as lamenting the disappearance of the yeoman farmer, Cobbett regretted the way in which the profits of commercial farming, and the social status which land-owning conveyed, had attracted men of little understanding of the duties and responsibilities of their privileged position. Since the passing of the Poor Law of 1597 able-bodied unemployed were dependent on their parish for poor relief. Being dependent on the poor rate had a demoralising effect on many labourers. Farmers knew that wages would be subsidised from the rates and refused to pay their workers properly. A worker knew that however hard he strove he could never earn a living wage. Seven shillings a week was the normal rate.

The 1790s saw a series of disastrous harvests combined with shortages occasioned by the wars with France (1799-1815). Prices, especially of corn, rose rapidly, causing hardship to many labourers – bread was their staple diet. Wheat sold for 34 shillings a quarter in 1780 and by 1800 it sold for 128 shillings a quarter. Wages remained static, and labourers could not afford to buy enough for their family needs. Philanthropists tried to help, and even officials such as magistrates decided that something should be done, if only to protect themselves from a Revolution like the one in France. Attempts to get farmers to increase wages were resisted – if they raised wages when the price of wheat was high, they would not be able to lower them again when the price of wheat fell. In 1795 a group of magistrates, discreet persons and clergymen met in Speen in Berkshire with the declared aim of fixing higher wages to be paid by farmers; but instead they fixed a minimum rate for subsistence, with wages supplemented if necessary by poor relief. This was to reflect the price of a gallon loaf. A man could have the equivalent of 3 gallon loaves a week, women and children 1½ gallons a week. 'When the gallon loaf of second flour weighing 8 lb 11 oz shall cost 1s. 0d. every poor and industrious man shall have for his own support 3s. 0d. a week either produced by his own or his family's labour or an allowance from the poor rates and for the support of his wife and every other in his family and so in proportion as the price of bread rises or falls, that is to say, 3d. to the man and 1d. to every other of the family on every penny which the loaf rises above a shilling.'

The minimum rate was soon adopted as a maximum. Large farmers paid half wages, the parish the rest to 'Speenhamland' levels. The practice, confirmed by Parliament in 1796, was widely followed in south east England. There was much abuse by employers of the new system and this resulted in a big increase in Poor Law expenditure.

The Napoleonic Wars left a legacy of poverty and unemployment. Soldiers were demobilised, others were released from war industries and there was little alternative work. The situation was aggravated by another series of bad harvests. The end of high wartime prices meant profits were cut and wages often reduced. Many smallholders had difficulty in supporting their families. Many able-bodied labourers depended on poor relief.

Chapter 10
The Lindfield Connection – Why Lindfield?

Lindfield's population in 1801 was 1,077. The area under acreage was 5,763. It was still very much a rural area, any trades being basically related to agriculture. There was little industry to mop up any unemployed farm labourers. At the end of the eighteenth century Sussex had the highest poor rates in England. Between 50% and 60% of families were poor. In 1803 23% of the population of Sussex received relief.[1]

In his book *Glimpses of our Ancestors in Sussex,* Charles Fleet described Lindfield in 1824 as 'eaten up with pauperism.'[2] Precise detailed records are missing for this period, but it appears that £500 per annum out of the poor rates was used at this time for the relief of able-bodied labourers and their families. Some in fact were receiving payment for looking after parish orphans. In 1801 it is recorded that some of the relief was given in kind, for example a pair of shoes, 1 shirt, cloth, 1 pair of sheets, even a hat.

According to Fleet: 'The absence, for a long period from the neighbourhood of Lindfield of any great family, the decay and disappearance of the original owners of Pax Hill, Board House and Wakehurst Place (the De La Bordes and Culpeppers) the dismantlement and virtual destruction of Kenwood's – the chief residence of the Chaloners and the desertion of East Mascalls (formerly the family home of the Newtons and Noyes) these factors have doubtless had their effect on the present state and even appearance of Lindfield. The decay of the old families left the lower classes without the protection, which they had enjoyed in earlier days. The Pelhams, who succeeded the Chaloners as Lords of the Manor of Lindfield lived at a distance and the landed interest in the place was not great.'[3] This final sentence is questionable as Thomas Pelham Earl of Chichester took an interest in Allen's Lindfield schemes.

At that time the Anglican church in Lindfield was not in a position to take a lead in addressing social issues. The living was very poor – the great tithes being owned by a lay impropriator. In 1758 the curate, in reply to a circular sent by the Archbishop of Canterbury, stated that he was allowed only £20 a year – although the annual value of the tithes was then £120. The Archbishop declined to interfere. Parishes at this time were often perfunctorily served and left to the ministration of underpaid curates and incumbents of poor livings. 'The history of the Church in Sussex during the eighteenth century differs little from that in any other county. It was a period of neglect and religious deadness, churches fell into disrepair and services

87

were slackly conducted.'[4] 'Education at Lindfield for the people there was none,' according to Fleet. If by this Fleet meant that there was no regular weekly school available to all, he was correct. In *Sussex Schools in the 18th Century*, John Caffyn provides details of four Lindfield schools:[5] Charles Baker established a small private grammar school in 1731 and John Wood had a boys' day school in 1735 – reading and writing was available for 6d. per week.

The following two advertisements appeared in the *Sussex Weekly Advertiser:* In November 1790 Mrs. Smith advertised her girls boarding school at Lindfield 'To open at CHRISTMAS next; Board, washing and lodging, with education. viz. English. French. and every branch of needlework, at FIFTEEN POUNDS and FIFTEEN SHILLINGS per annum. The use of the Globes, TWO POUNDS and TWO SHILLINGS per annum.' [This seems an expensive extra!] There was no entrance fee required; music, dancing, drawing and writing were extras at the usual rate.

At the beginning of 1793 Rev Henry Barwick opened a boys' boarding school at Lindfield: 'His plan is to take twelve young Gentlemen only and to qualify them for Business, the Public Schools, or University. His terms for English. TAUGHT GRAMMATICALLY. Writing, Accounts. Shorthand, Book-keeping, History, Geography, and Philosophy. Sixteen Guineas a year; the Classics, French, and Mathematics, Eighteen Guineas, and One Guinea entrance … Lindfield is a very healthy, pleasant Village, situate in a genteel and respectable neighbourhood. N.B. Mr. Barwick has had the honour (and he flatters himself with credit) of educating several of the Nobility, Gentry etc of this kingdom, during a period of upwards of twenty years.'

There are also references to two independent schoolmasters working in Lindfield: Stephen Vine, 1779, and March Pierce, a cripple, 1803. It is possible that these two schoolmasters took some pupils from the poorer classes if they could afford the fee. There is no mention of dame schools or charity schools in spite of the efforts of the Society for the Promotion of Christian Knowledge (SPCK). 'Children are made tractable and submissive by being early accustomed to Awe and Punishment and Dutiful Subjection. From such timely Discipline the Publick may expect Honest and Industrious Servants.' (An Account of Charity Schools lately erected 1708.) The eighteenth century promoters of charity schools often met with resistance from those classes whose financial support was necessary, and also with apathy from the poor who questioned the need for education.

The Sussex Weekly Advertiser carried a report on the Quarter Sessions held in Lewes in 1792. 'The chairman in his charge to the Grand Jury observed and lamented that of late felonies had much increased in this division of our County, and as a means of preventing them, in future, he recommended that "attention be given to Sunday Schools".'

The earliest reference to the establishment of a Sunday school was in 1814 when the Lindfield Sabbath school was set up by the Lindfield Congregational Church under Reverend Joseph Watson. According to C. Caplan, William Durrant, a brewer, helped to run the Sunday school. He also conducted an evening school for secular instruction during the week: 'It is a fact which ought to be noted to the honour of Mr. Durrant that when the Parish afforded no other means of religious and general instruction he came forward to subserve in combination with the preaching of the Gospel the moral and social elevation of the neighbourhood.'[6] Not long afterwards a resolution was passed at a parish meeting to open an Anglican Sunday school.

'February 23rd, Lindfield, 1818. Resolved at a General Meeting of the Parish Officers and Principle *[sic]* Inhabitants that the Sunday School be opened on Sunday next and that the children do assemble at the church and that James Shelley and Mrs. Nye be nominated as Master and Mistress to attend and receive them at the hour appointed and who shall receive a yearly salary for their trouble and attendance. Resolved that some of the respectable Inhabitants, both Ladies and Gentlemen be solicited to render assistance in instructing them. Resolved that a subscription be opened to defray the expenses of the same.'

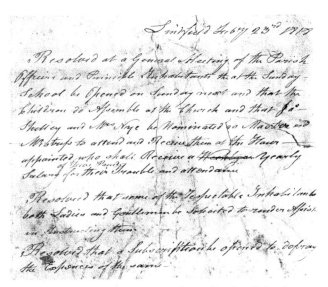

Resolution to open an Anglican Sunday School.
(West Sussex Record Office.)

89

Chapter 11
The Establishment of Schools of Industry and a Boarding School in Lindfield and their success

It appears that Allen looked for some time for a place where he could carry out his plans. In 1821 he spent some weeks in Brighton. He not only made inquiries himself into the state of the agricultural population but he also employed a person to visit neighbouring villages to gather further information, especially with reference to the instruction offered in Sunday Schools and other educational establishments. In 1824, after lodging at Brighton, Allen went to Lindfield to investigate the possibility of obtaining land for his School of Industry, calling upon several of the inhabitants to explain his views. According to his diary, he was generally well received but 'The people here are half a century behind some other places in intelligence.'[1] In his article Bartle wrote that 'the villagers were at first opposed to the industrial school believing that their children were going to be kidnapped and sent overseas' but he does not quote his source.[2] Allen met Stephen Wood who turned out to be a useful assistant. On his return to

Friends Meeting House, Ship Street, Brighton.
(Courtesy of Brighton Meeting.)

London he wrote: 'A very satisfactory and important journey.' Lindfield was still basically a conservative rural community. Some people would inevitably feel a prejudice and suspicion about a 'foreigner' and more particularly a Quaker. Allen must have seen it as a challenge. Tact and persuasive skills must have been necessary to secure support for his plans, not attributes which Allen always exhibited!

Earlier biographies give the impression that the school and allotments were all Allen's doing. However, wealthy patrons were also needed. In 1824 Allen discussed with the Earl of Chichester, Lord of the Manor of Lindfield and John Smith, MP, successively of Midhurst, Chichester and then for the County of Buckinghamshire, the acquisition of land at Lindfield for a School of Industry. They both promised their assistance. The aim was to provide education for the children of agricultural labourers to further their industry and independence. The Earl promised land opposite to the western side of the Common on Black Hill. Some earlier accounts suggest that Allen built the school and adjoining workshops all at his own expense. There is no evidence for this, although it seems likely that he was a main contributor. It was essential, before the introduction of state grants in 1833, and indeed even after 1833, to secure subscribers. When Ardingly, Sussex, opened its National School in 1848 it needed 53 subscribers, which, incidentally, included the Earl of Chichester who gave £10, and the Chichester Diocesan Association £30, in addition to a grant from the National Society of £30. Altogether £356. 9s. 6d. was raised.

The Lindfield establishment, which was opened in 1825 by the Earl of Chichester, was called 'the schools', as there were three teachers in three different rooms – for the infants, girls, and boys – unlike some of the early schools then on the monitorial system which had one large room for all the pupils. Teaching was conducted on the principles of the British and Foreign School Society. Although there were daily Bible readings, teaching was non-denominational. The schools were to be open to all: '… it is however expected that every child on the Sabbath, shall attend the place of worship to which its parents belong.' The fees were small – the use of monitors helped to keep down the expense.

Fleet provides a detailed account of the schools, which he visited in 1852.[3] They are unlikely to have changed much since Allen's time.

> 'These Schools are in as full and efficient operation now (1852) as when they were first founded. In 1851 they were attended by 175 children, who came from all parts of the neighbourhood – from Haywards Heath, Wivelsfield, Worth, Ardingly, and even as far as Ditchling – distances of three, four, five, and even six and seven

miles. On a fine morning – aye, and even when the sky looks black and threatening – you may meet the little travellers trudging along the country lanes and roads, with their dinners in their little baskets slung before them, with clean and cheerful faces, tiny clothes, and those rosy cheeks and blue eyes which attest their Saxon origin.

1824 Letter from Allen to an Esteemed Friend.
(Museum of the Royal Pharmaceutical Society of Great Britain.)

Question them and you will receive a ready answer, and a bow or a curtsey, by the fashion of which you may soon know a scholar of the Lindfield Schools. As nine o'clock approaches they gather together in front of the Schools – on the Common and on the wide roadsides, and at nine they enter the spacious schoolrooms, from the walls of which are suspended well selected lessons in which the great truths of Christianity are taught in the simplest and yet most sublime of language.

The Schools are divided into three compartments – the first and largest for the boys: the second, for the girls; the third, for the infants of both sexes. The system of instruction is adapted from that of Joseph Lancaster, and the copy-books of the lads, their slates, and their ready answers to questions in arithmetic, geography, &c., speak for the progress they make. The boys generally have an intelligent look, some of the elder ones have their little classes around them, and boys in round frocks, and with ruddy, rustic faces, such as one generally sees at the plough's tail, act the part of school-master to a little circle with a gravity and a readiness which prove them to be masters of their part. I asked the names of one or two of the boys, and soon found that it is not only the labouring classes who avail themselves of these schools. The sons of respectable tradesmen and of substantial farmers were seated at the same desk with the children of labourers. A day or two afterwards, falling into discourse with a farmer who has the reputation of being the 'heaviest' tenant-farmer in the parish, I found that he had a son at the Lindfield Schools, and he said the boy got on very well – better, he thought, than he had done at the Hurst College, from which he had taken him. I do not know what they teach at the Hurst College, or what the scholars pay; but at these Lindfield Schools, the boys are taught to write and read and cypher [do arithmetic] well – in the latter department they go as far as algebra, mensuration* &c., and they understand what they are taught; and for this education the boys pay 3d. per week; the girls, 2d.; and the infants, 1d. This rate, however, is reduced if there are more than one child in a family. Thus, if two attend from the same family, they pay only 2d. each; if three, only 1d. each; and if there are four, they pay nothing. So, too, as a premium for regular attendance, if a scholar attend every day in the week, he may claim his money back again. The above scale is so low that there are few labourers who cannot nowadays send their children to receive good English education.

---

* Measuring rules for finding lengths, areas and volumes.

Passing through the girls' room, where all is order and industry, we come to the Infant School – perhaps the most interesting of the whole. Here there were some 40 or 50 little things ranged in rows upon seats rising one above another at one end of the room: from the mere baby of eighteen months up to four or five years old. When one reflects upon the task of managing one child of such tender age

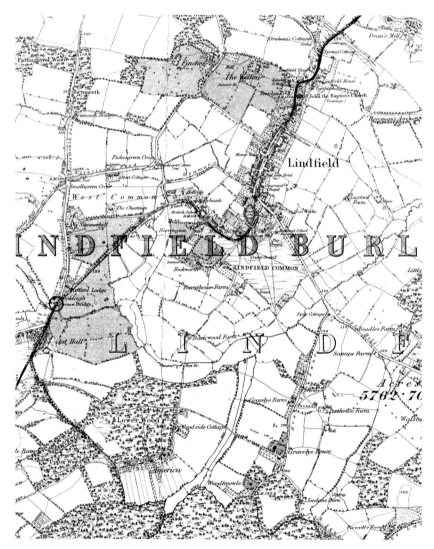

1874 Extract from Ordnance Survey Sheet XXVI. (West Sussex Record Office.)

– to say nothing of two or three – by what species of discipline can 40 or 50 be brought into anything like order? If, one would think, a 'reign of terror' were justifiable anywhere, it would be here. Yet, so far from this, there is an utter absence of all severity – all rigid discipline, all restraint or monotonous order – and yet there is no noise or disorder. The little things, boys and girls, little and big, sit together on tiers of seats, and are free to shift themselves about and indulge in that restlessness which is the characteristic of childhood, and to curb which is to torture them. They may vary their position – turn and twist about as much as they please. But the mode of instruction adopted is such as to satisfy this very restlessness, and to gratify that desire of motion and change which is peculiar to childhood. Either the little hands or the little feet are constantly in motion, or there is something for the eye to rest upon or the ear to listen to. Imitative action (acting, in a humble sense), rhymes, pictures, music – these are the agencies by which the mistress of the Infant School instructs and occupies her little pupils. As you enter, at a word they are all on their feet to welcome the lady or gentleman who is come to visit them. Then, the mistress, placing herself in front, repeats some rhyme, with suitable action, descriptive of the many familiar objects, or figures, or occupation about us, and a forest of little hands and arms are engaged – perhaps in describing circles, semi-circles, little parallel lines, &c., &c., which one wonders at seeing thus made a source of amusement, as they evidently were, to children scarcely able to hold up their little arms. Some little things, unable to keep up with their elder and more advanced school-fellows, showed their sense of the fun by clapping their little hands together; and one, more ambitious than the rest, in a desperate attempt to illustrate "This is what I do when I tie my shoe," turned a summersault right over, displaying as sturdy a pair of legs as ever carried so little a body. How strongly these games interested the children was shown by a little incident which fell under my notice, and which I cannot help telling, though I fear it is a terrible breach of confidence. When the game commenced, the mistress observed that one of the youngest infants – "Baby Saxby" she called her – was amusing herself by sucking a piece of pipe which she had brought in with her from the play-ground. "Put that down, baby Saxby" said the mistress, and baby Saxby's hand instantly disappeared behind her, and her large blue eyes were fixed upon the mistress, who very quietly took the pipe away from baby Saxby and went on with the game. But I had noticed what the mistress had not – that baby Saxby had a piece of pipe in each hand, and no sooner was the mistress's eye off than up went the pipe again to the little mouth, and baby Saxby looked as if she had half-a-mind to be a naughty baby. But as the game went on, and as the children proceeded to describe "This is the way the miller goes," &c., baby Saxby got so thoroughly interested in the part she was playing, and into such good humour with herself and all her baby-world, that, by-and-by, she stepped out of her place, and, going up to the mistress with the other piece of pipe in her little hand, laid it on the table. The good genius of the game had triumphed over the evil genius of the tobacco-pipe! Then there was a march round the room, after the mistress, still repeating instructive rhymes; and then, the infants resuming their seats, one

CURRICULA PROVIDED IN CERTAIN SCHOOLS OF INDUSTRY

SCHOOL	CURRICULA																	
	R	W	A	RK	PS	G	S	K	WV	SN	SB	C	N	L	P	AL	T	DL
1 Bagshot											X							
2 Bamburgh Castle	X	X	X	X	X		X	X			X							X
3 Bath							X	X			X							
4 Birmingham						X					X	X			X	X		X
5 Brentford					X						X							
6 Bolton											X							
7 Brighton											X	X					X	X
8 Cheltenham							X	X			X							X
9 Chester									X									
10 Fincham (Norfolk)	X	X									X							
11 Hertingfordbury (Herts)						X					X							
12 Kendall	X	X			X	X	X	X			X		X				X	X
13 Leeds											X							X
14 Lindfield (Sussex)	X	X	X	X			X	X			X	X		X		X	X	X
15 Lindsey					X													
16 Liverpool	X	X	X				X					X						
17 City of London	X	X	X	X							X		X				X	X
18 King Street, Golden Square	X	X		X			X				X							X
19 Lewisham	X					X	X	X										
20 St Marlebone	X	X					X	X							X	X		
21 Nottingham	X	X									X							
22 Oakham	X						X	X			X							
23 Potton (Beds)	X	X	X								X					X		X
24 Rutland						X												
25 Spratton (Northants)														X				
26 Sunderland	X	X									X							
27 York	X						X	X			X							

KEY

R	Reading	S	Spinning	N	Net making
W	Writing	K	Knitting	L	Lace making
A	Arithmetic	WV	Weaving	P	Pin making
RK	Religious knowledge	SN	Sewing/Needlework	AL	Agricultural labour
PS	Psalmody	SB	Straw platting/Basket making	T	Trades
G	Geography	C	Card setting	DL	Domestic labour

Curricula provided in certain Schools of Industry [4] *1780-1840. (History of Education Society.)*

bright-looking little fellow, some three years of age, was invited to test his powers of spelling, which they did by putting words to him which would have staggered many an elder scholar, and I could scarcely believe my ears as I heard one little urchin of four or five require another still younger to spell elephant, rhinoceros, and even hippopotamus, each of which was rattled off, with a vast number of other words of smaller calibre, as quickly as they were put. Then a slate was produced, on which the visitors were invited to write what figures they pleased, in tens or hundreds, and no sooner were the figures chalked up than a dozen little figures were signalling their eagerness to answer. Questions in addition and division were equally well resolved, by boys and girls – and all with the most evident delight and without the slightest appearance of envy. The girls were less forward than the boys in offering to answer questions, but when called on by the mistress they were equally quick in replying. Some of the children were perfect specimens of Saxon beauty – large blue eyes, flaxen hair, and cheeks as red and white as the softest peach. One or two, however, were little dark gipsy beauties, with sloe-black eyes and raven hair. All the time these exercise were going on, one little thing was snuggled up in one corner of the room on a bed which is always kept for children too young to keep awake during the hours of school.'

The concept of the industrial school was not forgotten – even the infants were set tasks such as plaiting straw baskets and hats and doing patchwork. As in Hannah More's schools, the girls did spinning, weaving, knitting, needlework and domestic duties. As the boys grew older they were given training in printing, gardening, farming, woodwork, simple metal work, shoe repairing or cloth manufacture. The boys who learnt about the printing trade assisted in the production of *The Lindfield Reporter* or *Philanthropic Magazine* – 'being a repository for Hints and Suggestions calculated to promote the comfort and happiness of man.' Brief notes were given of philanthropic and benevolent activities in all parts of the world, with articles on domestic issues such as the amelioration of the criminal code, the importance of allotments and the emphasis on fair wages so that labourers could be independent of parish assistance. Allen was the editor and contributed many articles. As well as teaching a trade to those engaged in its production, it was a way of gaining publicity for various charitable concerns. Copies of *The Lindfield Reporter* were given free to subscribers to the Lindfield Schools and sold for four pence to non-subscribers. On the initiative of Allen, much of the printing for the Society of Friends at this time was also done in Lindfield by boys from Allen's industrial schools.

Some interesting insights into the Lindfield Schools are provided by Christine Alsop (née Majolier) in her memorials. On a number of occasions she was left in charge of arrangements at Gravelye House and in the Schools, when Allen was travelling abroad:

> 'I found much to occupy my time. I went every morning and afternoon to the schools, about a mile off, attending also to the printing office, which was worked by the elder boys of the school, under William Eade. The correcting of the proofs was a work of patience indeed, as there were often as many mistakes as words (!). The schools were not then on so good a footing as they acquired afterwards; the master and mistresses were inefficient, and yet I had to keep everything going, and send as fair an account as I could to William Allen.'

During the summer months things were reasonably pleasant with occasional visits from her Brighton friends besides sometimes going there to 'meeting'. With winter she could be lonely. She tried to occupy herself by translating J. Gurney's *Portable Evidence of Christianity* into French, and by learning Greek in order to read the New Testament in the original. She also kept the accounts, exchanged the weekly despatches to and from London, taught an old cottager to read, and comforted Elizabeth Wood in her final illness. Certainly life was not always easy:

> 'The winter of 1832-33, which I spent at Lindfield, was cold and damp. I was now for the first time exposed to the extremities of an English climate. In the early part of the winter I took cold; but not considering it of much importance I continued my exertions, not-withstanding the exposure to which my occupations subjected me. With a constant cough, I still went to the schools daily, and stood for hours in the school-rooms, and the printing office; took my dinner with S Farrand by the side of the school fire; returned home for tea through rain, mud, frost, or snow; and spent a great part of the evening in correcting damp proofs from the printing office, which had to be read over a great number of times. For half-an-hour in the evening I had two adult pupils. I afterwards attended to the accounts. It was no wonder that my health gave way, and that a foundation was then laid for the delicacy of chest to which I have ever since been subject. It was, I own, through imprudence on my part, for I am sure William Allen would have been the last person to wish me thus to injure my health; but I was then young, buoyant, and extremely desirous to serve my beloved friend. I had no doubt I should lose my cough in the spring, and I thought I should soon be well again when I had time for a little nursing.

Spring came, and I had no relief. I applied blisters to my chest, but still went to the printing office and read the proofs. At last some of my kind friends, particularly Susanna Kemp, of Brighton, urged me to inform William Allen of the real state I was in. I did so, and left Lindfield for medical advice, expecting to return after the Yearly Meeting to resume my post; but it was ordered otherwise. The means resorted to were ineffectual in removing the cough, and I rapidly lost strength. Serious apprehensions were entertained, and intimated to be by the medical men who were consulted, that my

THE

HISTORY

OF

RICHARD MAC READY,

THE FARMER LAD.

———ooo•cooo•✤•cooocooo———

———oooocooo•✤•cooocooo———

Lindfield:

PRINTED BY C. GREENE, AT THE SCHOOLS OF INDUSTRY.
Sold by Harvey and Darton, Gracechurch Street, London.

1832.

Title Page – The History of Richard Macready. The Farmer's Lad. (Glimpses of our Ancestors in Sussex. 2nd Series. C. Fleet.)

lungs were in a diseased state, and that a return, to my native air, at least for a time, was the only thing from which I could expect relief, so that my life might be preserved a few years longer.' [5]

Christine returned to France in 1833.

According to a report on the Lindfield Day Schools in the January 1838 edition of *The Lindfield Reporter:*

'The average attendance throughout the year is about 100, but considerably more receive the benefit of the schools, as the children of labourers are frequently kept from attending regularly when their labour is wanted by their parents; and as many children are kept from school entirely because their parents are so poor that they make their children earn what they can, and because they do not estimate the value of instruction. The proprietor has desired the master of the boys' school to offer at the rate of 2d. or 3d. per day for each boy who will labour two or three hours upon land and attend two or three hours at school. He has set apart about seven acres of land, on which the master, William Backshell, employs these boys; it is called Backshell's Farm, and a distinct account is kept of it. It began at the time called Michaelmas, 1837: the result to be given next year, if nothing unforeseen present.

EXPENSE OF THE DAY SCHOOLS FOR 1837.

	£. s. d.		£. s. d.
William Backshell, Master, 14s. per week	36 8 0	Payments with some of the children	13 5 6
Sophia his wife, mistress of the girls school, 10s. per week	26 0 0	Deduct the last quarter of the master's salary as it is charged to his Farm as above………	12 13 8
Charlotte Verrall, mistress of the infant school, 12s. per week	31 4 0	Deficiency …………..	80 6 1
Taxes, &c	7 2 3		
Coals	5 11 0		
No rent charged			
	106 5 3		106 5 3

Was Allen an Educational Innovator?

Allen's attitude to Owen's plans for a secular school environment indicate that he was not an innovator. The idea of schools of industry has a long history. John Locke, in his report to the Board of Trade in 1697, proposed schools which combined occupational labour and schooling for children on poor relief. Produced in 1792, Clara Reeve's *Plans of Education* outlined a scheme for reducing dependence on relief. The SPCK advocated uniting manual work with religious instruction. As early as 1695, the Quaker John Bellers published a pamphlet entitled *Proposals for a Colledge [sic] of Industry*. Francis Place showed a copy to Robert Owen who in turn circulated 1000 copies of it in 1818. It is almost certain that Allen would have seen a copy or heard it discussed. He may have been influenced by William Corston's industrial school in Norfolk or Lancaster's agricultural school at Maiden Bradley in Somerset – although this ran into problems. There was a printing press at the Borough Road school. There were Quaker industrial schools in other parts of the country, and examples abroad such as the industrial schools of Russia and Fellenburg's Poor school in Switzerland and, as mentioned, the ideas and work of Sarah Trimmer.

Allen's Personal Involvement

However, the fact that he was not an innovator does in no way belittle his individual achievement. Allen remained involved in the Lindfield schools for the rest of his life, as his diary entries reveal. 1827 references show that during the summer and autumn he frequently spent a week or two at his cottage in Lindfield, generally accompanied by his wife and two of her nieces.

> 1836: 'Sixth month 24th. At the schools in the morning.[6] Twelfth month 21st. At Lindfield, rose a quarter past five, read Exodus. Walked to meeting. I addressed the children on the fear of God and had peace.' [7]

> 1837: 'Eighth month 5th. Samuel Gurney and his daughter Sarah with Elizabeth J. Fry and her daughter Catherine spent some hours with us very agreeably. They seem much pleased with what they have seen and before they left us, E.J.F. was engaged in prayer for us and for the establishment.[8] Twelfth month 13th. Again E.J.F. and P. Bedford visited the schools.' [9]

When Frederick Hill visited Lindfield in 1831 there were 300 children on the school books but attendance was irregular. There was obviously considerable fluctuation in numbers. An 1835 reference suggests 150 pupils on the register. The average daily attendance was 100. Some children came a considerable way and brought their dinners. Parental needs were not forgotten. There was a lending library in the school house and, when they were in Lindfield, Allen and his wife taught villagers to read and write – holding a weekly class for this purpose. A large number of parents were not able to read or write.

In 1834, after a visit to Ireland, Allen set up another school in Lindfield 'where a select number of boys might be received as boarders upon low terms ... each boy to have a separate sleeping room.' The boys were to be sent over from Ireland and 'are to be employed in cultivating land under a person well skilled in husbandry ... They are to be taught to do everything for themselves ... to make their own beds and to keep their own apartments clean. They are to be taught reading, writing, arithmetic, English grammar, Geography, land measuring ... and they will have the use of a select library. Care is to be taken that they be well instructed in the knowledge of the Holy Scriptures, in the evidences of the Christian religion and in the principles of the Society of Friends. Ten pounds are to be paid with every boy upon admission, for board, lodging, clothing etc. for one year.'[10] A master was to be appointed to run the school. The Lindfield boarding school was a private venture unconnected with the BFSS and supported by Quaker acquaintances in Ireland. Correspondence and the diaries again reveal Allen's close involvement. He wrote to a friend in 1836: 'Our boarding school here prospers and is a source of real comfort to us. There are now thirteen lads; they all appear very happy and are obviously improving in every respect. We frequently have them and their superintendent to take tea with us, when we enter in to free and familiar conversation. They all keep diaries of the employment of their time. I generally give them some lectures on Chemistry or Natural Philosophy, when I am down [from London].[11] 1838 Eighth month 27th. I had three of the boys to tea this evening and took them into my study separately, to have some religious conversation with them; it was very satisfactory and afforded peace to my own mind. Afterwards showed them Saturn, the Moon, etc through the large telescope.[12] 11th month 27th. We have now 17 boarders – this evening they all came to tea which I enjoyed very much. Addressed them on religious subjects and their conduct.'[13]

A lighter note is the reference to having allowed the boys 'to play at cricket in my field.'[14] After his final continental tour in 1840 he was relieved to find that 'the school seems to have managed well in my absence. There are now 21 boarders and I was comforted with the appearance of the children.'[15] He retained an interest in the boys from the boarding school even after they left Lindfield. To two of them he wrote: 'It will be a great comfort to me that you continue steady. Avoid bad company, love retirement and continue to set apart a quarter of an hour or more every day for the duties of religion.'

A Report on the Progress of the Manual Labour Schools in Lindfield appeared in *The Lindfield Reporter* in January 1838. Seven boys had left the boarding school in 1837 – five had returned to Ireland. Most had spent two years at the schools. The intention was to give the pupils, especially those from Ireland, a taste for 'the useful and honourable employment of Agriculture as one of the most independent methods of procuring a livelihood.' It was a cause of great regret when the relations or friends preferred a place for them behind a counter or a situation as a clerk.

A daily diary was kept to show what proportion of time was spent on each activity. The following daily average was made up from the reports of the examinations for the year 1837:

	h.	m.
Reading, Spelling, Writing, Arithmetic, Grammar	2	49
Reading History, Natural Philosophy, Travels &c.		21
Private and optional reading of the Holy Scriptures, The lowest 17 minutes and highest 27 minutes		18
Private religious reading, also optional, the least 18 minutes, and highest 42 minutes		28
Geography, use of Globes &c.		24
Agricultural employments	3	23
Various other work		34
Public reading of Scriptures &c.		50
Private religious meditation in silence		15
Total Daily Average	9	22

The habit of thus accounting for the employment of time is calculated to teach the pupil its value, while it presents a subject for profitable retrospection.

Details of the Boys Gardens then followed. They were a generous eighth of an acre and each boy was permitted to cultivate half in potatoes and half in corn, for his own profit as pocket money.

14 Gardens { 12 Rods   Wheat or   168 Rods   35 Bushels
             12 Rods   Potatoes   168 Rods   301 Bushels

When the amount for manure, seed, rent &c. was deducted, the share of each boy was in the proportion to the produce of his garden and they received as under:

	£	s.	d.	At the rate per week for a whole year d.
B. Doyle	2	0	0	9
Walker	1	15	9	8
Kirk	1	11	9	7
Faren	1	6	9	6
White	1	12	11	7½
Keen	1	7	5	6¼
Shepherd	1	6	7	6
Pim	1	1	9	5
Mullin	1	2	4	5
J. Doyle	1	6	4	6
Macquillen	1	3	1	5¼
Fry	1	2	0	5
Duvally	1	11	3	7
Moran	1	16	11	8½

Amounting in the whole to £20 4s. 10d.

Most of the boys reaped the wheat themselves, and put it up in sheaves.

There followed a report on the Boys farms – 12 boys had ¾ acre each to farm and two, 1½ acres. A detailed list of all the crops and valuations was submitted in the typical methodical style of Allen: 'It is highly probable that the ground being now brought into a regular train and properly cultivated, the crops next season will be still more abundant.' No allowances were made for poor seasons and consequent bad harvests.

The accounts for the boarding school for the year 1837 are included.

Debits
Provisions

	£.	s.	d.
Wheat and bread	62	10	5
Meat	31	19	9
Milk, 4292 qrts	17	17	8
Fish		6	9
Potatoes	3	16	0
Rice	2	9	7
Butter and cheese	3	6	5
Sugar	2	18	6
Sundries	1	17	4

	£.	s.	d.
	127	2	5
Clothing	20	4	4
Tools	4	2	3
Coach hire	1	9	11
Candles	3	5	7
Soap	1	11	6
Stationery and books	2	15	8
Coals, &c.	9	3	6
Superintendent's salary	52	0	0
Female assistant	10	13	0
Part of the wages of the Agricultural Labour to teach the boys	5	2	0
Sundries	6	0	2
	£243	10	4

Credits

Value of boys' labour as compared with the same work done by a man who should be paid 12s. per week.

	£	s.	d.
1st, 2nd and 3rd months	8	10	6
4th, 5th and 6th months	11	12	3
7th, 8th and 9th months	12	1	0
10th, 11th and 12th months	13	0	9
Paid by or due from pupil's friends	163	13	6
Deficiency	34	12	4
	£243	10	4

The article acknowledged that full accounts are not given as vegetables and fruit from the garden were provided free and no charge was made for rent or repairs – these were covered by Allen and subscribers.

Chapter 12
Allen's Plan for District Schools

Allen's intention, which was not fulfilled, was that the Lindfield schools should be models for others. His plan for District Schools was outlined in *The Lindfield Reporter* or *Philanthropic Magazine* in (August) 1837. The article provides a useful insight into the progress of the schools and into his detailed plans for the future and recognised the need to obtain benefactors, co-operative farmers and tactful visitors. It is of interest that children as young as two were to be included in the survey.

'ON THE PROGRESS AND PRESENT STATE OF THE MANUAL LABOUR SCHOOLS AT LINDFIELD IN SUSSEX. In the number for the first month (January) 1836, we gave notice of a boarding school at Lindfield, in which the boys were employed for a certain portion of their time in manual labour, principally in the cultivation of land: the number of Pupils was twelve, it has been increased to fourteen. The experiment has proved most satisfactory; four of the pupils having been about two years in the establishment, and qualified for usefulness, are returned to their friends in Ireland, and their places have been supplied by others; it is the object of the Proprietor to make it as much as possible a sort of Normal School, in which lads and young men may become qualified to superintend similar schools, or be useful to such benevolent persons, as may desire to make allotments of land; and considering the great advantages likely to result from this plan, he is now desirous to receive the help of such of his friends as may be inclined to assist him in the extension of the benefits of his schools to a greater number. The manner in which the pupils dig and manage their land, has given great satisfaction to competent judges, while their progress in different branches of learning has been in general highly satisfactory; some of them have learned the use of the sextant and theodolite, are well versed in geography and are acquainted with several branches of useful knowledge; some have been taught to make shoes and considerable attention is paid to their religious instruction. It may be interesting to some readers to be made acquainted with the cost of the establishment for the year 1836, no charge being made for rent of premises, containing an excellent well stocked garden or for the fitting up and furniture of the bedrooms &c. which amounted to above £260. The Superintendent and female assistant board with the family.

Provisions

	£	s.	d.		£	s.	d.
Meat	27	1	3				
Milk	14	17	0				
Wheat &c.	43	2	2				
Rice	1	12	6				
Potatoes	15	11	9				
Sugar &c.	2	7	8				
Butter and cheese	1	9	4				
Vegetables &c. bought	2	11	4				
Carried over					108	13	0
Brought over					108	13	0
Superintendent					52	0	0
Assistant and Agricultural labourer To teach the boys					39	8	10
Coals					26	12	2
Tools					6	13	1
Clothing, much of which was made in the Establishment, as Drill, Shoes, &c. several Presents having been also received					16	16	1
Soap					2	1	10
Washing					3	19	5
Sundries, Stationery, &c.					14	8	7
					£270	13	0
Estimated value of boys' labour					50	13	2
					£219	19	10

The number of pupils was twelve in the fore part of the year, and fourteen in the latter part. Average 12½. About £17 10s. each.

It is the intention of the Proprietor, if funds can be obtained, to increase the number of pupils to twenty.

The day School for Boys, that for Girls, and that for Infants, are kept up; the daily average attendance last year was about 100, but this does not show the extent of the benefit; for the parents of many children being poor, and some not duly appreciating the value of education, the attendance is very irregular, so that the number actually receiving instruction may be about 150.

The expenses of the day schools, including the salaries of the Master, the Mistress of the Girls school, and the Mistress of the Infant school, amounted in the year 1836 to £103. 7s.10d. Some of the children come from a considerable distance, and bring their dinners with them.

Mention was made in the article, in a former number above alluded to, that the Boarders had allotments of land adjoining to the Schools of 26 rods each, which they were permitted to cultivate in corn and potatoes, and to apply the proceeds of the sales to their own use as pocket-money. The crops both of wheat and potatoes are very fine this year, and the ground was in nearly all cases entirely cultivated by themselves in their own time; the exact value however cannot be ascertained until about two months hence, but we purpose to state it in a future number.

Each of the Boys who is of a suitable age, has a plot of ground consisting at least of three quarters of an acre or 120 rods, called a Boys Farm, which is divided into 24 compartments, in which are cultivated precisely those articles a poor man ought to raise who was to get his living from five acres of land, on the spade-husbandry plan: they thus become acquainted with the time of sowing, planting, manuring, &c. and with the amount of the products. There are twelve of these farms, and about once in a month or six weeks an account is taken of the state of each division, which is noted in a book.

It is part of the plan to render the lads as independent as possible of extraneous assistance; they scour their bedrooms, and as much as may be do every thing for themselves; one in turn is waiter every week, and one assistant.

From the experience already obtained, the Proprietor is convinced, that in a district where there is a sufficient population, it would be in the power of benevolent individuals, resident within a square of 16 miles, to establish schools, so that the children from the remotest parts would not have to walk much more than two miles to school. He has divided the map of the County of Sussex into 101 squares, each running four miles North and South, and four miles from West to East. It is designed to begin with those, where from the residence of liberal minded persons, there is the greatest probability of success; and as there is already a central school in the 55th square, in which Lindfield is situated, the proposed organisation of this division may serve as a model; the square is subdivided into 16 equal parts, each of which includes of course one square mile. The first thing to be done, will be to form an association of all the benevolent persons who may be disposed to promote and complete the great work of the education of all the poor children IN THE SQUARE; the first inquiry of course must be after such, the next object will be the division of labour, by appointing visitors in every district of a square mile, where practicable; each of these to be provided with a book containing heads of inquiry; these books to be brought to the Committee, which should meet at the most convenient central place. Teachers of Sabbath schools would be very desirable for the office of visitors. This duty should always be performed in a delicate way, so as not to hurt the feelings of the poor.

The following are the heads of inquiry for Lindfield square, Number of villages or hamlets, and in what part of the square situated – and how many inhabitants.

North

1	5	9	13
River Farm Little Naldry Great Naldry Copyhold Boardhill	Avens Kenwards	Hill House Busstey Farm Buckshalls Farm	Godards Little Plummerden
2	6	10	14
Penns Wickham Mill	Finches Sunt Farm	Paxhill Lindfield o Schools Lower Walsted	Mid. Plummerden Lower Plummerden Cockense East Maskells Mill
3	7	11	15
Hardens Fullers Butlers Green Little Haywards Great Haywards	Gravely Colony	Walsted Common Beadles Hill Cuddles	Walsted Farm Nether Walsted
4	8	12	16
Haywards Heath Record	Birch Green Hurst Farm	Cuthedge Lywood Common Colwell Slingwash	Upper Hookland Lower Hookland Abrook

West / East

South

The 55th Square – The Lindfield Schools. The Lindfield Reporter 1837.
(Library of the Religious Society of Friends in Britain.)

Heads of Inquiries.
1st Population of District.
2nd How many schools already existing, of what kind, boys, girls, infants, Sabbath schools, average number attending, and how much paid per week with the children.
3rd How many children above two years of age without education.
4th Wages of agricultural labourers.
5th Have they any allotments of land, what quantity to each, and how cultivated.
6th Names of the principal farmers in each square, the number of acres they hold, the number of labourers they employ, which of them are liberal men, and allow their labourers land.
7th What persons of influence reside in the square, the names of those who are considered to be benevolent and liberally disposed.
8th Is there any Benevolent Society, or Bible Society in the square.

The visitors of Districts would render valuable assistance to their central school, by encouraging parents to send their children, and by inquiring after absentees; a list of whom should be furnished to each Visitor every week.

In this manner the active benevolence contained within the limits of every 16 square miles, would be concentrated upon a definite and practicable object; and the good results of it would ever be before the eyes of those engaged in a work, so philanthropic, patriotic, and truly Christian.'

To show that it was possible, given favourable circumstances, to form an agricultural school in the middle of sixteen square miles, a small tract was published, entitled *Hints for Establishing Schools of Industry in Agricultural Districts at a small expense, by the Proprietor of the Lindfield Schools*. The tract was intended to show that three cows might be kept on the produce of five acres and that the boys might cultivate such an area while at the same time they were receiving a good education. It had been proved that eight stout boys on the spade husbandry plan, working only from two to three hours a day (which is less than what was actually practised in the Lindfield Schools) would easily be sufficient for the purpose. Allen's plans for other schools never came to fruition. Did he run out of time and energy? Did he find the prospect of acquiring a sufficient number of wealthy subscribers to support his schemes too daunting? Certainly to date there is no evidence of other industrial schools within the sixteen square miles of Lindfield. It is not known whether the tract influenced reformers elsewhere.

Chapter 13

The Anglican Alternative – The Lindfield Schools 1832-2000

In 1832, the East Sussex National Society sent a form to the Anglican minister in Lindfield, posing the following questions:

'How many children attend the Established Church as members of Sunday or weekly schools supported by church funds?

'Have you any school already in union with the National Society for the education of the poor on the principles of the Established Church?

'How many day scholars and how many Sunday scholars are there?'

The 1833 Education Act provided £20,000 a year towards the cost of school buildings – grants were awarded where half the building costs had already been raised by voluntary subscription. With its system of funding through its dioceses and parishes, the Church of England National Society was to prove far more effective than the British Society at raising money – between 1833 and 1838 the National Society acquired 70% of the annual grants. The Anglican Church was putting its house in order and was anxious to extend its influence through the education of the poor. By the end of the 1850s there were seventeen times as many National Schools as there were British Schools. However, Lindfield continued to present problems for the local Anglican church. The 1832 form currently held in the West Sussex Record Office was not completed. Was it simply a matter that, once a British School had been established, there was less incentive to open a National School? This seems to conflict with the rivalry between different religious groups elsewhere. Was it a reflection on the poor state of the Anglican church in Lindfield? As late as the mid-nineteenth century, church income from rectorial tithes was only £35 and no contribution was made by the lay impropriator. In an 1851 census, the vicar stated in his report to the Ecclesiastical Commissioners that the parish 'calls loudly for government interference.' Was this an indication of poverty and lack of wealthy church ratepayers? In fact a National School opened on the Common in 1851. It was built on land conveyed by the third Earl of Chichester 'to the minister and church wardens of Lindfield upon trust to permit the erection of buildings for the education of children and adults or children only, of the labouring, manufacturing and other poor classes of the parish of Lindfield.'

The school was housed in what became known as the Reading Room, later the Social Centre. Unfortunately, very few records of this school appear to have survived, but it seems to have struggled and even had periods when it closed altogether. Was it during one of its closures that the enthusiastic Reverend F. Hill Sewell, vicar for most of the period 1839-62, opened St John's Parish School, a day and Sunday school, situated opposite the church; or did he want to have an Anglican school in traditional close proximity to the church? According to Helena Hall, Sewell's school carried on for some years, but there are no records of numbers and, as the school was never conveyed to the church authorities, it ceased on his death in 1862, pupils moving to the National School on the Common. The National School continued to flounder. It closed, then re-opened in 1865. At the end of the year there were only thirty pupils. The teachers were dismissed. Was it merely because the school was unpopular – its position on a low part of the common being regarded as damp and unhealthy; or did the existence of the well regarded British Schools on Black Hill make an alternative unnecessary? Kelly's Directory, published in 1866, made no mention of a National school in Lindfield. It referred only to the schools opened by Allen on Black Hill: 'They have for many years been the means of furnishing a sound and Scriptural education to the children of the labouring and independent classes of Lindfield and its vicinity.' There were 223 pupils, half were Anglicans and half were Dissenters. The schools were still supported by voluntary subscriptions.

In 1875 the Jubilee of Allen's Black Hill British Schools took place. Six hundred parents, friends and scholars assembled for speeches and tea in a large tent put up in a field at the back of the school ground. A small presentation copy of a short life of William Allen was printed by the Religious Society of Friends to commemorate the Jubilee.

The period 1861-1880 in Lindfield saw a decline in the influence of the local Congregational Church. With the growth of a new Congregational Church in Haywards Heath there was a more limited catchment area. There were a number of internal disputes and disruptions, with seven pastors presiding in the period 1861-1880, and financial support was less secure. The Black Hill Schools found it less easy to secure voluntary subscriptions. Forster's Education Act of 1870 decreed that primary education should be available for all. New Board Schools, paid for out of local rates, were to fill the gaps. In 1881 the British Schools on Black Hill closed, and a School Board of five was elected to supervise the establishment of a Board School. Thomas Wells, Headmaster of the Black Hill schools, saw through the transition, and the buildings on Black Hill and the Social Centre were used until the Victorian red brick building in Lewes Road was completed in 1883. The subscribers of the Lindfield British Schools voted that a sum of £200 – the result of legacies left so long as the schools continued – should be transferred to the new Board School. The fund was to be in memory of William Allen. The interest was to be devoted yearly to prizes given for proficiency in Scripture Knowledge. The fund was vested in the new school in perpetuity and so it has continued, through the various educational changes which followed, until it was transferred to the new Lindfield Primary School, opened at Beckworth in 2000. Thus the William Allen Prize Memorial Fund is a connecting link between Lindfield's educational past and present.

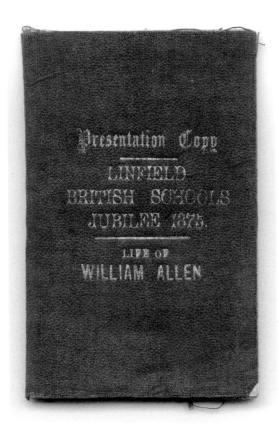

A presentation copy of
Linfield [sic] British Schools Jubilee 1875.
Life of William Allen.
(Lindfield Parish Council archives.)

It is a fitting tribute to the work of William Allen on behalf of Lindfield children that the main hall of the new Lindfield Primary School has been named the William Allen Hall.

No trace remains of the main school building of Allen's schools, as it was pulled down in 1898 and two houses were built on the land. However, the Master's house, now called Little Pelham, is still in existence. The old dormitories and workshops have been converted into the six Pelham Place cottages.

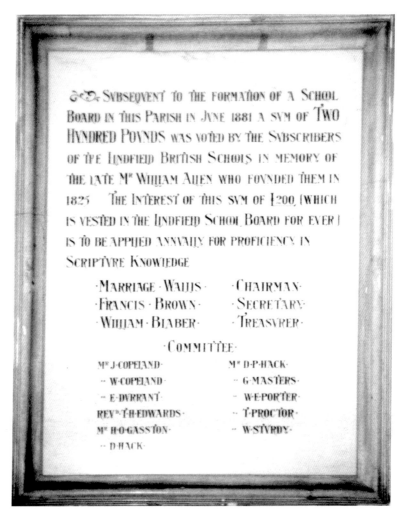

Memorial Board to William Allen. (Lindfield Primary School.)

Pelham Place cottages, formerly workshops and dormitories, as they are today. (Claudia Gaukroger.)

The former schoolmaster's house, now Little Pelham. (George Murrell.)

Chapter 14
The Lindfield Allotments

In 1827 Allen wrote and published a pamphlet entitled *Colonies at Home or The Means for Rendering the Industrious Labourer Independent of Parish Relief and for providing for the Poor Population of Ireland by the cultivation of soil.* The aim of 'his' Allotment System was:

'1. To wean the poor from dependence upon the parish and to put them in the way of providing for all their wants by their own industry.

2. To enable them to procure an education for their children in moral, religious and industrious habits.

3. To raise such a moral independent feeling in the Poor as may induce them to consider it a disgrace and shame to receive alms from the parish and to engage in marriage until they shall have made a reasonable provision for a family.

Every poor rural family should be provided with a small piece of ground and instructed in the means of cultivating it to the greatest advantage so that each labourer could supplement the wages received from his employer.'

The pamphlet gave a list of crops to grow, a guide to the four-year rotation of crops, the importance of manure, the quantity of food necessary, the treatment of a cow and the design of the labourers' cottages and outbuildings. The loan of a small capital would be essential and must be provided by local benefactors. 'Home Colonies' were a remedy for poverty far superior to emigration. This, it was suggested, merely removed the best and left the worst. By best Allen meant those with motivation. The pamphlet of some thirty pages ran into several editions. Allen not only needed local supporters, he was anxious to interest influential people further afield in his scheme for land settlement. He chose Lindfield as the place for a demonstration of its practicability as it tied in with his plans for industrial schools and his awareness of the condition of the local labourers.

Although it is convenient to refer to 'his' allotment system (as earlier authors have all done), Allen himself was aware that he was not an innovator. The pamphlet admits that he is 'corresponding with persons of experience in different parts of the country on the best appropriation of the land and the best plan for the cottages. I have obtained much valuable information in this way.' Philanthropists in all parts of the country were aware of the very real distress of rural labourers. William Corston had produced a pamphlet advocating the government purchase of land for the benefit of the poor. Arthur Young, who had written *Annals of Agriculture*, arguing that enclosures were an economic necessity, now supported the setting up of a Scarcity Committee – the idea advocated being that the state should provide seed potatoes for the poor to plant in plots provided by landlords. A similar plea that landowners should give some enclosed land for allotments and grazing was put forward by the Bettering Society. In 1817 Robert Owen's Report to the Committee for the Relief of the Manufacturing Poor argued that, instead of Poor Relief, the government should raise a fund to establish village settlements of about 1,200 inhabitants who would be given land to produce their own food. In fact since the later Middle Ages numerous haphazard attempts had been made to provide and enclose common land and allot it to the needy poor.[1] In the early nineteenth century a number of well-intentioned landowners and churchwardens in many parishes had attempted to establish allotments, but such efforts had been scattered and spasmodic. Not surprisingly, considerable opposition came from many landowners and farmers who objected in principle to the idea of sacrificing their land. Demands were made to limit the size of allotment lest too large a parcel might take up the whole of a labourer's time (and if he was able to make a living he would be less anxious to work for a landowner). A further objection was that allotments could tie the labourer and so interfere with the mobility of labour. The economist John Stuart Mill argued that allotments were a 'method of making people grow their own poor rates.'[2] Supporters argued that it stopped the drift to towns. Helena Hall referred to 'His new experiment – the Allotment system.' It was a new experiment for Lindfield; although Allen was not the originator of the allotment concept, full credit must be given to him for realising a well thought out scheme and at an early date. Feargus O'Connor's National Land Company, set up to build rural settlements with four acre small holdings for industrial workers, did not come into being until 1845, when the General Enclosure Act gave powers to commissioners to provide for the landless poor in the form of 'field gardens' limited to a quarter of an acre each.

How the Lindfield Allotments were Set Up and Managed

Allen would not have been successful in pursuing his aim of establishing allotments without the assistance of influential members of the community – notably Thomas Pelham, Earl of Chichester (involved also in the grant of land for the Black Hill Schools) and his son Henry Pelham who succeeded to the title in 1826, well known as 'a patron of good and charitable works.'[3] John Smith MP was also to play a significant role, although in the minds of local people, then and since, the credit for the experiment has gone entirely to Allen. In fairness to Allen, it must be said that without his enthusiasm and drive others would not have responded. John Smith, impressed by the schools, bought the estate at Gravelye and Scamp's totalling about 100 acres on the south side of the common, and he placed some of the land at Allen's disposal. Earlier biographers suggested that there was financial assistance from the Earl of Chichester, but it was more likely to have been a moral and social contribution.[4] Although Allen himself appears to have put money into his twin projects, that is, the schools and allotments, from the beginning he saw the need to gain support, in all senses of the word, from the wealthier inhabitants of the parish. He called personally on many of them, although his proposals were at first greeted with suspicion and apathy. According to Christine Majolier (Alsop), Allen 'had many difficulties and discouragements to contend with, only known to those who were intimately connected with him.'[5] In a second edition of *Colonies at Home* Allen wrote of the strong opposition and deep rooted prejudices that he had faced in Lindfield. There was 'a narrow minded view of self interest in some farmers and others': as parish officers, some were in the position of voting on poor relief which could save £40 or £50 a year in wages, allowing them to buy labour at a lower rate (in effect the Speenhamland System).

It was Allen's own enthusiasm that led to the setting up of a cottage society to finance both his projects. Money was needed to provide small loans for labourers and to finance the building of cottages which appear to have been designed by Allen himself. When an elderly labourer, Stephen Wood, decided to offer assistance, this helped to sooth any qualms amongst the labourers. Eighteen cottages were built with an acre and a quarter of land to each. There were six cottages in each set – the rents being two shillings and six pence and three shillings a week. In Gravelye Lane seven other cottages were built for smallholders with 5-6 acres of ground, each able to support a cow and a pig. A small house was built for Allen's own use on his visits to Lindfield. Fleet visited the cottages in 1852 and described them in a series of articles in the *Brighton Herald*:[6]

> 'I visited one of each class, beginning with the lowest – the 2s. a week tenements. They are long, low, thatched cottages, with a good-sized kitchen, and three bedrooms connected by a long passage – all on the ground floor. These cottages are only one room deep, and have no staircase. The inconvenience is, the length of the house – 50 or 60 feet, and the distance between the extreme rooms. This is

remedied in the second or 2s. 6d a-week cottages, the rooms of which are two deep, and so lie more compactly together. The outhouses to both consist of bake-house (with good oven and copper), wood-house, piggery, well, washhouse, &c., with plenty of spare room at the back; whilst in front run the long slips of ground, averaging an acre to each, cultivated either as garden or arable ground – with fruit trees, or wheat, beans, vegetables, &c.

In one of the 2s. tenements I spoke to a woman – healthy and strong – who said she had been a widow five years, and had brought up nine children – two were with her now. She had grown wheat upon part of her ground, and there was the produce in a neat little stack; and there were beans, &c., for the two fat pigs in the sty. She said she could manage to keep herself pretty well with her pigs, her fruit, her bees, &c., though this year the help she needed cost her more than usual. She seemed cheerful and contented. Her next-door neighbour – an intelligent looking, tidily clad man, of about 40 – was standing at his door. He got, he said, 12s. a-week as a labourer, and said he did not see why a man should have less than 2s. a-day. From enquiries I had made in other quarters, I found that 10s. was the average wages in the neighbourhood, and in winter 9s. or 1s. 6d. a-day. But the men who got these wages were not in a situation, like our friend of the Colony, to demand higher; they had not, like him, an acre of good land to fall back upon; they must either take the 9s. or 10s., go to 'the house' or starve.

The next set of cottages, at 2s. 6d. a-week, are much superior to the 2s. tenements. They are slate-roofed, with stuccoed fronts, instead of mere mud and beach [sic]; and their rooms, though all on the ground floor, are, as I have said, two deep. These tenements, like the other sets, stand by themselves, and are built two and two – each couple in the form of a T – the down-stroke representing the outhouses – woodhouse, bakehouse, piggery, wash-house, &c. – facing each way, so that one building provides outhouses for two tenements. These are strongly built and well arranged. So are the cottages themselves. I went into one at random. The mistress of the house – a good-looking woman – was busily engaged in drying her clothes (the day having been wet), and being surrounded by half a dozen children, who had just come from school, she was, as might be supposed, in a little bit of a pother (fluster) – yet all was clean and neat; the woman was cheerful; the children happy; and there was that unmistakable air of comfort which bespeaks abundance. The wife opened the doors of the sleeping-rooms – three in number – and the bed-hanging and bed-clothes were as white as snow. The husband showed me his woodhouse and piggery and garden – the latter full of fine fruit trees, planted chiefly by himself. Half his garden was so occupied; the produce of the other half stood in the shape of a plump little stack of wheat. He had grown, he said, two quarters on half-an-acre. He intended to thrash it himself, and smiled when I asked if he sent any to market. He had, he said, seven children, and they did not let any crumbs fall under the table. He, too, had held his tenement from the time of William Allen, and spoke of him as in the like of whom he did not expect to meet in this world.

Passing on to the third set of cottages, 3s. a week, which stand on a higher elevation, on a line with Gravelye House [the former residence of William Allen, but at this time, 1852, the residence of the Rev. Mr Johnson, the Incumbent of Lindfield], a still higher degree of comfort met the eye. These cottages are such as any member of the middle ranks might be happy to occupy – indeed, two of them were now tenanted by respectable tradesmen; but the others were still occupied by the original occupants, and one of these, Edward Cook, was a labourer on Gravelye Farm when William Allen bought it, and went from the farm to his present home, in which he has brought up seven or eight children, now all out and settled but one, who lives with his parents. Edward Cook is still a healthy, stalwart man, with handsome features, and of frank, open address. When asked by my companion (a patriarch of the village) what he thought of William Allen, he replied "What do I think of William Allen? Why, William Allen was the best man that ever I knew. He was the poor man's friend. Many a time has William Allen come to me and said 'Well, Edward, dost thee want a little money?' Mayhap I did, but I couldn't tell when I could pay it back again. 'Never mind that, Edward; there is £10, and after harvest I dare say thee will be able to pay it.' And he would never ask me for it again, though I always found a way to pay the money, in bits." So spoke Edward Cook. I should observe that this tenant rented seven acres of land in addition to the acre attached to his house. It was a rule with William Allen that a man should have as much land as he could cultivate properly, but then, to ensure proper cultivation, these extra acres were let at the usual rent, 30s. an acre; and of these Cook had, and still has, seven – consisting of a meadow and some cornfields, to raise oats for his horses – he being a carter.

I was anxious to know what kind of land the "colony" was when it was first planted; and my companion told me an anecdote illustrative of the point. After Farmer Simmonds – who must have been a shrewd old customer – had sold the land to William Allen (or to John

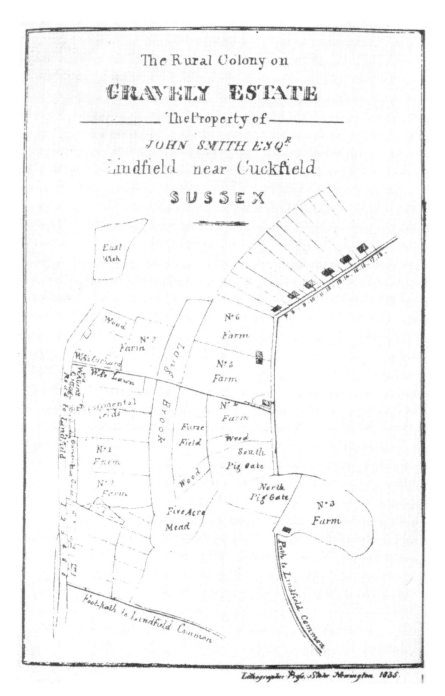

The Rural Colony on Gravely [sic] Estate. (Country Life, 22/11/1956.)

Smith, Member for Bucks, and father of John Abel Smith, MP for Chichester – for not even the tenants of the land or the builder of the cottages ever exactly knew which was the owner – William Allen or John Smith – such bosom-friends were they) – but when Farmer Simmonds had sold Gravelye Farm, he said to William Allen, pointing to the land between Bent's Wood and Sergisons Wood, down which run the plots of the Colony, "The best thing you can do with that, Sir, be to turn out colts on it. 'Tis a hungry soil, and eats up everything you put into it, and makes no return. It owes me £200, does that piece of land." The object, however, of the purchaser was to turn out men – independent men – working for themselves, upon it, and not colts. Perhaps he recollected the saying of Arthur Young – "That a sure holding will turn a rock into a garden; an insecure, a garden into a desert;" for though the land was not given in fee to the occupants of it, nor is it even held on lease, yet the rent was never raised, nor was the tenant ever disturbed during good conduct. The estate passed away, at the death of William Allen, into the hands of the Rev. Mr Scutt, and is now held by his son-in-law, the Rev. Mr Johnson, Incumbent of Lindfield; but, to the honour of that gentleman be it said, the colonists remain undisturbed – many, indeed, work for him – and the rent of their cottages and ground is the same as that paid to the founder. However, whether William Allen thought of Arthur Young or not, he turned out his men, and the place only fit

Gravelye Lane about 1914.
(Postcard courtesy of Peter Duncan.)

for colts was soon converted into a garden. Not that he left all to the tenants' unaided efforts. Allen was a practical chemist; he preceded Liebig in the application of science to the cultivation of the land. He had a pit in which he tested various substances as manure, as whale's blubber, &c., and the land of the Colony had, doubtless, the benefit of his experiments, as the tenants had of his counsels and encouragement. Was there an empty pigsty? "What! No pig?" said the kind-hearted old man, "thee must have a pig." And lo! There was a grunting in the stye. After another visit, the village shoemaker (I have his word for it) would suddenly make his appearance in the Colony, and begin measuring the ill-shod feet of half-a-dozen children. He had his orders, and no bill was ever sent in to the parents – no name breathed.

From his house at Gravelye, William Allen looked down on his Colony, and it flourished beneath his eye; for he appealed to the best feelings of Englishmen – the love of home and independence; and I believe it is a fact that no member of the Colony ever went to the parish for relief.' [7]

Much of the land does seem to have been poor in quality, but as a scientist Allen was undaunted. He had already carried out experiments with allotments for the poor in Stoke Newington. He would also have been familiar with the work of 'Turnip' Townshend and his four course rotation of crops (wheat, turnips, barley and clover) used to improve soil and boost crop yields in Norfolk by the introduction of grasses and roots. In addition Arthur Young had produced a lot of information about crop rotation, drainage, marling to improve sandy soils and hoeing.

An article, entitled Rural Colonies at Lindfield related the terms of the tenant agreements:[8]

> 'All the tenants must sign an agreement to the following effect, acknowledging that they may be dispossessed of their cottage and land, if they do not fulfil it: To observe moral conduct: not to suffer any spirituous liquors to be sold on the premises, nor used in their families, except for the purpose of medicine: to send their children to school: to cultivate with the spade, on the plan laid down for them, or not to vary without leave: not to underlet or take lodgers without leave: with other covenants as to manure, &c., and to give quiet possession, upon due notice; it being understood that the rent is not to be raised, nor they turned out, so long as they comply with the conditions, except under extraordinary circumstances. They are to keep no horse without leave. The success which has attended these allotments is very great, considering the virulent opposition of

some farmers and others in the neighbourhood who got great part of their work done by the parish paupers, and also two unfavourable seasons, and the low price of produce, about 40 per cent under what it was a few years ago, – this is particularly felt by the cottagers in the article of pigs.

Samuel Gurney, of Lombard Street, London, and Upton in Essex, has joined in promoting these objects at Lindfield, by purchasing the Estate called Scamps or Penns, near that of Gravely. This little Estate has for some years past been let out to poor persons, who have derived great benefit from the allotments, – it will in future be pretty much cultivated by twelve boys, to be boarded in the Schools of Industry, for whom provision is just made.'

There then follows an interesting section on possible future developments:

'The plans now in operation at Lindfield are applicable to many important purposes: for instance: – If Government were to grant crown-lands in Ireland, under certain regulations, much of the misery now existing among the peasantry there might be remedied.

Schools of Industry and Agriculture might be supported on the plan, for poor orphans and other children; in which they might be made to provide food and clothing for themselves, and at the same time receive a useful education.

Workhouses in country places might, in great measure, be supported on the plan. A sufficient allotment of land being provided, the inmates might be made to contribute largely to their own support.

Reformatories or Penitentiaries, for juvenile and other criminals, might be established upon the plan with great effect, when an enlightened policy shall adopt systems for the prevention of crime and the reformation of criminals, instead of resorting to the barbarous and criminal expedient of extermination.

And lastly, the general adoption of these plans would nearly annihilate the poors' rates in agricultural districts.

The object for publishing what has been done and is now doing in the Lindfield colony, is to encourage landed proprietors who have hearts to feel for the poor, and who only want to be informed of a practicable plan for their relief, "to go and do likewise;" and we may rely upon it, that wherever the whole of the farmers' labourers in a parish can be thus accommodated, not only might the poors' rates be reduced to a mere trifle, but what is of still greater importance, the moral character of the poor will be raised; and that state of degradation which leads to vice, and consequently to misery, would be exchanged for one of independence and self-respect: a state most

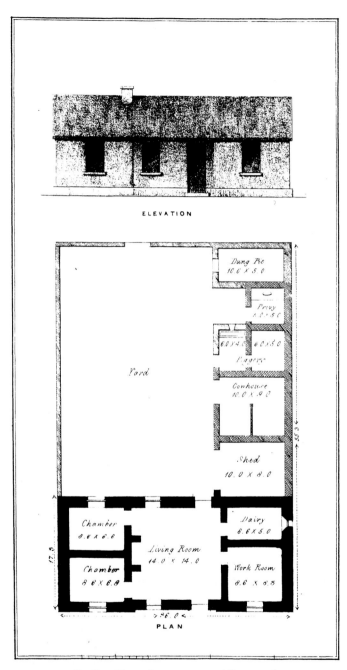

*Outline Plan of a cottage and farmyard.
(Colonies at Home pamphlet.)*

favourable to virtue, and consequently to happiness. The fires of the Incendiary would then no longer blaze, nor the shortsighted politician any longer be employed in the vain endeavour to extinguish them with blood.'

On the completion of the cottages Fleet relates that: 'Mr. Allen went to a parish meeting and told the parish officers that he had built some cottages and wanted tenants for them, and that the tenants he wanted were industrious men with large families, and he didn't care how large the family was, provided the man was industrious. This, it need hardly be observed, was the very class who were the recipients of parish relief. One man and his family had had above £80 in three years; he became a tenant of the "Colony", and from that day forward he ceased to be a pauper. Others followed; for there was a comfortable home and land to be had for a mere trifle, and the strongest love of an Englishman is, for a home and land. And so, in a short time, all the tenements of what was by some called "The Colony", and by others "America", were occupied, and a social revolution commenced in Lindfield.' In a later paragraph Fleet adds: 'One condition the tenants of the "Colony" amply fulfilled: they all had tremendous families – six, seven, eight, nine, and even ten and twelve children. It is so still: children swarm in the "Colony" to such an extent that it has been nicknamed "the Warren" ' (1852).[9]

Fleet refers to the Colony but it is not clear how quickly this term came into use. The word was of course used in Allen's pamphlet, 'Colonies at Home'. Fayle, writing in 1884, refers to a conversation he had in the train to Brighton with a young American traveller. He suggested that they left the train at Haywards Heath and travelled to Gravelye House – 'the favourite residence of the George Washington of these parts [i.e. Allen]' and then to 'a land of promise to some generations in its small way – as your big continent is to thousands of thousands from the Old World at this day – the allotment colony of America.'[10] When did the expression America as it referred to this part of the locality arise? It is not possible to date its usage, but maps of the area from 1870 onwards use the term. Helena Hall stated that it was nicknamed America in fun, but a more serious note is suggested. The Lindfield experiment was like a small America to the people of the area. According to Armytage, 'the cottages were so delectable in the light of living conditions elsewhere that his settlement was nicknamed America.'[11] Colonies were seen as a way for the poor to have a fresh opportunity in life which was also the intention of home allotments. The same pioneering spirit found among American settlers was needed here. In their book *The Story of Haywards Heath*, Ford and Rogers suggest that, situated on the

*Gravelye Cottages, Lindfield, c.1908.
(Postcard courtesy of Peter Duncan.)*

*Gravelye Cottages, Lindfield, c.1908.
(Postcard courtesy of Peter Duncan.)*

Gravelye Cottages, Lindfield, c.1912.
(Postcard courtesy of Peter Duncan.)

THE MID SUSSEX LAUNDRY, LINDFIELD

Aerial view of The Mid-Sussex Laundry, Lindfield.
Showing some of the allotment gardens, late 1920s.
(Postcard courtesy of Peter Duncan.)

edge of the parish and away from the village community, the paupers in question may be said to have been 'sent to America'; but in the days when people were accustomed to walking long distances the colony was perhaps not all that remote.

Publication of Allen's Schemes

Allen's views received wide publicity, partly the result of his own energetic efforts. *Colonies at Home* went into a second edition in 1832, which, translated into other languages, had separate detailed provisions on the growing of potatoes, carrots, parsnips, turnips, cabbage, red clover, lucerne, mangel wurzel, yellow beet, wheat, rye, barley, oats, buckwheat and Indian corn or maize.

Some supporters pointed to the good results achieved on the Lindfield allotments and argued that, if his scheme was universally adopted, poor rates in agricultural districts might be reduced to a comparative trifle. In the first report of the Sussex Association for bettering the condition of agricultural labourers, it was stated that the produce over four years of single acre allotments, after all expenses of extra labour, rent and manure were deducted, showed a clear profit of 2 to 3 shillings a week. A hard working labourer might make 4 shillings a week (if manure was used and the hire of extra labour was avoided). The garden plot should support a pig. Allen looked upon the pig as the poor man's friend. From his pig he would obtain 'a revenue of a shilling a week or more to be deposited in a savings bank.'

In 1833 another pamphlet was published: *A Plan for Diminishing the Poor Rates in Agricultural Districts – being a brief account of the objects and plans pursued upon Gravelye estate in the parish of Lindfield by John Smith MP and William Allen for bettering the condition of the agricultural poor*. Many well known people visited Allen's colony, including Lord Brougham the Lord Chancellor, Lord John Russell, Robert Owen, and William Wilberforce. The Duke of Sussex, son of George III, also paid him a visit and a diary entry notes: '… with his accustomed affability and kindness [he] mingled in the family circle at Gravelye and partook of some light refreshment.'

According to Fayle, 'the social revolution spread throughout the district. The cottages were superior to the labourers' hovels of the time. Adjacent parishes felt the influence of the "colony" in the moral and physical condition of their labouring classes.'[12]

Two articles provide further details of the management and intentions of the allotments. The first, entitled *Rural Colony at Lindfield*,[13] starts with a reference to the 1834 Poor Law Amendment Act which abolished out door relief. In future no able-bodied labourer could gain assistance unless he was willing to enter a workhouse. The full extent of the unpopularity of the new workhouses was yet to emerge. At this stage Allen hoped that the new arrangements would improve the economic position of the agricultural labourer, especially in Sussex and some of the Southern Counties where 'they had been degraded to the state of paupers and while receiving parish relief, have been hired at the rate of one shilling, eight pence, sixpence and even three pence a day. If distress was initially caused by the new arrangements, then a voluntary association should be set up to raise a fund, purchase land, and pay the labourer a minimum two shillings a day or the equal in piece work. A sub-committee should supervise the work and the committee should meet one evening a week to pay the labourers and receive progress reports.'

The article went on to show how the land cultivated should make a profit, the labourer who was better clothed and fed having more strength and spirit for work. 'A labourer on a 5 to 6 acre farm, following crop rotation, should be able to pay his rent and by gradual annual instalments repay any loan. Experience has shown that the following are the best adapted to provide a successful plan:

Rye, to be sown in Autumn, and cut green Spring	60 lb per rod
Red Clover	200 lb per do.
Lucern [sic]	200 lb per do.
Artificial Grasses	200 lb per do.
Cabbage	200 lb per do.
Yellow Beet Leaves	150 lb per do.
Chicory	200 lb per do.
Symphetum Asperimum, or Prickly Comfrey	200 lb per do.
Indian Corn, to be cut green	200 lb per do.
Spring Tares [types of vetch]	120 lb per do.
Winter Tares	120 lb per do
ROOTS FOR WINTER	
Potatoes	120 lb per do.
Yellow Beet Root	150 lb per do.
Swedish Turnips	150 lb per do.
Carrots	150 lb per do.
Parsnips	150 lb per do.

The food must be cut and carried to the Cows.'

According to an extract entitled *Five-Acre Farms at Lindfield*, the project was successful:[14]

'In our number for the second month, (February,) 1835, the means are stated by which a sober, industrious, and intelligent poor man may support himself and family in high comfort, by cultivating about five acres of land by spade husbandry IN THE MANNER THERE RECOMMENDED. Most of the farms upon that plan at Lindfield, are now giving proof of the efficacy of the plans; the crops are abundant, and they have secured their corn, peas, seed, tares, &c.: the boys' farms are also flourishing.

'When we assert that five acres are sufficient for a man and his family, it is only upon the understanding that it is to be upon the Lindfield or garden plan, and under the inspection of a person well acquainted with it. Thus if we find a poor man with the qualifications above stated, we may proceed in this way: allow him from 12 to 14s. per week, keep an exact account of all expenditure for rent, taxes, seed, manure, and wages, and when the harvest comes, credit the farm with all the crops, and pay over the surplus to the labourer. This plan is now being acted upon at Lindfield, and we hope in a future number to give satisfactory results. We have clearly ascertained that with good management, the crops will more than pay for the labour and all expenses. The five acres may be laid down for the first year, either half in potatoes and half in corn, or in the following crops distributed over 32 divisions of 25 rods each. Three cows may be kept the first year, as soon as the crops advance sufficiently. John Smith Esq. of Dale Park, who is also proprietor of the Gravely Estate at Lindfield, has ordered his head gardener to lay down five acres of land upon this plan, on his estate at Dale: we shall look forward to the result of this experiment with great interest: the gardener is an intelligent and experienced Scotchman. It is very desirable to have these small farms carried on in various parts of the kingdom, and a comparison made of the products under the different circumstances.'

CROPS FOR A FIVE ACRE FARM.

	Divisions.	Rods.	Per Rod.	Green food.	Roots.
Rye to be cut green For Cows in spring	6	150	60 lb	9000 lb	
Potatoes after Winter Tares	8	200	2 bushels 120 lb	24000 lb	300 bushels.
Swedish Turnips after			2 bushels		400 bushels
Yellow Beet, Leaves	2	50	150 lb	7500 lb	
Roots			150 lb		7500 lb.
Turnip rooted Cabbage	4	100	60 lb	6000 lb	
Roots			1 bushel		100 bushels.
Drumhead Cabbage	1	25	200 lb	5000 lb	
Carrots	4	100	2 bushels		200 bushels.
Wheat	3	75			
Barley, 1st division with Red Clover under And the second with Saintfoin under.	2	50			
Prickly Comfrey	1	25			
Lucern	1	25			
	32 Div.	800 Rods = 5 Acres			

The red clover, saintfoin, comfrey, and lucern, cannot be calculated upon till the second year.

We shall probably return to this subject again in a future number, and for the present only say, that all persons subscribing ten shillings and upwards, will be entitled to five numbers of the Lindfield Reporter every month for the year in which the subscription shall be made. Subscriptions will be received by Cornelius Hanbury, Plough Court, Lombard Street, and London.'

Allen spent considerable time encouraging a wide circulation for his schemes. He corresponded with interested parties at home and abroad. He visited agricultural settlements in Germany and Russia. He made several visits to Ireland in the 1820s, being aware of the enormous problem of poverty among rural labourers. In his first edition of *Colonies at Home* he noted that 'in consequence of an erroneous opinion that there is a surplus population in Ireland, encouragement is given to emigration which is not necessary.' He went on to say that 'the deplorable condition of the peasantry in Ireland has long been considered a national disgrace plus the situation of agricultural labourers in some counties of England. Low wages led to demoralisation and an increase in poaching and theft.' However, he was sometimes so zealous in promoting his plans that he overlooked the difficulties of adapting them to other areas and people. As Maria Edgeworth pointed out to him in a letter of January 1827:[15]

'Dear Sir,

I am gratified and honoured by your sending me an account of your benevolent plans for Ireland, and I heartily wish you and them success.

There can be no doubt that what you call colonization at home, would be preferable to colonization abroad, if it can be carried into effect, because it would, in the first place, save all the risk, expense and suffering of emigration, and would, in the next place, secure to the home country the benefits of increased and improved cultivation and civilization. Your plans of improved agriculture and economy, appear most feasible and most promising on paper; but I fear that in attempting to carry them into execution in this country, there would be found obstacles of which you can form no estimate, without a more intimate knowledge of the habits of the peasantry of Ireland, that a *first* visit to this country could afford, or, in short, anything but long residence could give. Their want of habits of punctuality and order, would embarrass you at every step, and prevent your carrying into effect those regular plans in which it is essential that they must join, for their own advantage. Your *dairy plans* for instance, which have succeeded so well in Switzerland, would not do in this country, at least, not without a century's experiments. Paddy would *fall* to disputing with the *dairyman*, would go to law with him for his share of the *common* cow's milk, or for her *trespassing*, or he would pledge his eighth or sixteenth part of *her* for his rent, or his bottle of whisky, and the cow would be pounded and *re-pledged*, and re-pounded and bailed and *canted*: and things impossible for you to foresee, perhaps impossible for your English imagination to conceive, would happen to the cow and the dairyman. In all your attempts to serve my poor dear countrymen, you would find, that whilst you were *demonstrating* to them what would be their greatest advantage, they would be always making out a short cut, not a royal road, but a bog-road to their own *by*-objects. Paddy would be most grateful, most sincerely, warmly grateful, to you, and would bless your honour, and your honour's honour, with all his heart; but he would, nevertheless, not scruple on every practicable occasion, to cheat, I will not say, – that is a coarse word, – but to circumvent you; at every turn you would find Paddy trying to walk round you, begging your honour's pardon – hat off, bowing to the ground to you – all the while laughing in your face if you found him out, and, if he outwitted you, loving you all the better for being such an innocent.

Seriously, there is no doubt that the Irish people would, like all other people, learn honesty, punctuality, order, and economy, with proper motives and proper training, and in due time, but do not leave *time* out of your account. Very sorry should I be, either in jest or earnest, to discourage any of that enthusiasm of benevolence which animates you in their favour. But, as Paddy himself would say, Sure, it is better to be disappointed in the beginning, than the end. Each failure in attempts to do good in this country, discourages the friends of humanity, and encourages the railers, scoffers, and croakers, and puts us back in hope, perhaps half a century: therefore, think well before you begin and begin upon a small scale, which you may extend as you please afterwards. You may, in some happy instances, find generous, rich, and judicious landlords, who will assist you; but do not depend upon it, that this will be general, else you will be cruelly disappointed, not in promise, but in performance.'

How Successful were the Allotments?

Writing in 1830 Allen stated: 'My object in taking Gravelye Farm was to prove, by an experiment under the public eye, that it is possible to render the agricultural labourer independent of parish relief, even with his present very low wages by letting him have a little land upon fair terms and directing him in the cultivation of it. This experiment has succeeded.'[16]

In 1834 he noted: 'I leave Lindfield this time with a pleasing conviction that all the tenants are in a way to pay their rents.'[17] A diary entry in 1836 notes: 'At Lindfield. Took a walk to the Upper Colony. I was delighted to see all the cottagers' gardens in a flourishing state; some are extending them into the field.'[18] According to Perry, writing in 1935, there was a rapid decrease in the poor relief paid in the parish and a corresponding increasing in the self-respect of the labourers. Helena Hall went further and stated that no member of the colony went to the parish for relief.

Was the Lindfield experiment in fact an enthusiast's dream? Allen himself admitted to some misgivings. In 1834 he felt that it was 'very possible that I am too sanguine. We must feel warm upon our projects – otherwise from the discouragements we are sure to meet with here, they will drop through.'[19] In 1824, a clergyman, Sydney Smith,[20] wrote to Allen expressing his doubts about the Lindfield experiment:

'Suppose 3 Divisions A. B. C., an acre each:
A Turnips Potatoes & Garden stuff as these crops are pulled a batch of Winter Tares to come in very early for soiling next year.
B Winter Tares – Summer tares, Broad Clover – or as Green Food for soiling.
C Wheat ... and so on.

I suppose the animals to be a pig and a Cow – or two pigs and a Cow. If the acre of Green food would more than suffice then take out of B ¼ of an acre of Barley – otherwise Barley must be bought.

There would not be enough Wheat for such a family – but I know not how to play the game better –

When first I became Rector of Foston the poor people had no Gardens. I took 2 acres from the Glebe & divided them into 16 gardens – they pay me a fair rent & pay me very punctually. It enables them to keep a pig and they are supplied with Garden Stuff, they can gather together enough manure for so small a plot of ground. Early in a Summer's Morning or late in a Summer's Evening you may see before and after the hours of agricultural labour the whole population of the hamlet, man, woman & Child toiling in the public Gardens. I often see the best intended Schemes for the assistance of the poor ending in disappointment. I have no doubt (after an experience of some years) of the utility of Scheme ... I am quite unacquainted with the Garden Cultivation applied to Grain Crops ... The whole resolves itself into a question of Expense. – The Spade & the Rake (expenses apart) are superior Tools to the plough and the Harrow. They can make Land fine – deeper & with greater accuracy – and in Crops which do not require *all* the power of these Tools – of Course the power may be restrained – and the Land left in as Coarse a State as will suffice for the object ... I have seen no instances of Land in such quantities as 3 acres allotted to the poor. I have not heard anything upon the Subject – from a general conviction of the impracticable nature of such projects.

It appears to me as irrational as giving them Looms to weave their Clothes or Forges to make their Tools – it sins against the doctrine of dividing Labour – Such schemes are often laid before the public in the first Honeymoon of the Experiment & nothing is told of their subsequent failure ... Still I am open to Conviction and am very willing to suppose that you have anticipated and answered these objections, – and that you are well acquainted with the low state of talent & morals of the objects you relieve and of the serious obstacles their imperfections will occasion to your Benevolent Schemes ... I hope observations are not intended to extinguish

Charity but to prevent the disappointments of charity and to preserve its spirit ... If I can be of any use command me ... If you come into Yorkshire come & pay me a visit. I shall be very glad to see you.' [21]

In 1884 the 3rd Earl of Chichester wrote retrospectively for Fayle in reply to his inquiries respecting Gravelye and William Allen:

'I believe I am correct in stating that the property was purchased by John Smith, and rented by William Allen, for the purpose of carrying on his system of cottage farms. I think I am correct in this, because I well remember Mr. Smith saying to me (long after I had been in constant communication with W.A., and after frequent visits to Gravelye and the cottage farms) – "William Allen tells me that the experiment is very successful, but he never pays *me* any rent. He shows me a balance sheet, and then asks to lay out the rent due in building more cottages!"

I know not of whom John Smith purchased the estate, but it was sold after Allen's death to Mr. Scott.

I had a sincere and affectionate regard for William Allen, and spent many happy and interesting days with him. But I always thought that he deceived himself as to the success of these little farms.

I have at times carefully looked over his ledger, which was beautifully kept; but I also carefully inspected the farms, sometimes

William Allen cottage, Gravelye Lane.
(Lindfield Past and Present. Helena Hall.)

with an agricultural friend. I could never discover that there was a profit to the tenants. The crops appeared barely sufficient to pay for the labour.

I consider the chief cause of failure was the difficulty of obtaining sufficient manure. My own half-acre allotments failed also from the cause above mentioned. After fifty years' experience of cottage farming, I am convinced that unless the tenant can keep a cow or a horse, he will always fail for want of sufficient manure.

For ordinary labourers I find that a quarter of an acre *adjoining the cottage* is the most profitable arrangement. In all the instances on my own property where what may be termed cottage farms succeed, there is a horse and a cow, or two cows kept, or the tenant has some other means of earning a livelihood.' [22]

A letter to Fayle from Charles Fleet echoed these views: 'The experiment was doubtless a success, socially and morally, but whether financially is open to doubt.' [23]

Fayle, who normally defended Allen, must have been reluctant to publish these statements in his book on 'The Spitalfields Genius'. He had to admit that 'in a sense, William Allen did not make even Plough Court pay; that is, he was always spending in good works the money which he made.'

William Allen's house in Gravelye Lane as it is today (with extension).
(By courtesy of Marie and Peter Jones.)

Certainly there was no quick improvement. In 1831 it was estimated that £1,200 had been spent by the parish officers in one year in Lindfield on the support of 215 paupers, a hundred of whom were able bodied.[24] After the Poor Law Amendment Act in 1834 wages were so low that the commissioners found it impossible to abolish outdoor relief for able bodied men, and it was only very slowly that wages rose to replace the reduced poor law relief payments. The widespread employment of women and children led to frequent unemployment for men and helped to keep wages down.

In the vicinity of Lindfield there was no industrial area or major canal construction to mop up surplus labour. It was not until the coming of railways and the growth of new towns with opportunities such as bricklaying, plastering and the opening up of shops that surplus labour was to find a market. Basically the condition of the agricultural labourer in the 30s and 40s remained very wretched. In 1826 a Select Committee on Emigration had advocated voluntary emigration as a solution to the problems of excess labour at home and the needs of the colonies for labour. Between 1815 and 1826 there were six ventures in state aided emigration and the Poor Law Amendment Act of 1834 assisted some 25,000 paupers, chiefly agricultural labourers, from the S.E. of England to emigrate to Australia or Canada by 1860. It is not known how many, if any, left from Lindfield.

The last cottage was pulled down in the 1950s to make way for new development. (The Metropolis of Mid Sussex. W. K. Ford and A. C. Gabe.)

Traditional barriers to mobility were still strong – a poor standard of education, low incomes, family loyalties, the old settlement laws under which a pauper needing assistance applied to his own parish, all impeded freedom of movement, but some families probably left in search of a better life nevertheless.

In 1937 the allotment cottages were condemned under a demolition order. The smaller ones were demolished in 1944 and the remaining ones in the 1950s. Helena Hall was shown round one of the larger cottages in 1958. It had a porch at the side able to house a pram, a kitchen scullery with a good brick oven, and a little sitting room. A flight of thirteen rather narrow steep stairs led to three small bedrooms. But although the cottages have gone, local road names bear witness to the esteem in which Allen was held in the area. William Allen Lane, Hanbury Lane and Allen Road provide a direct link, whilst names such as America Lane, New England Road, Washington Road, Boston Road, Mayflower Road and Penn Crescent relate to the American settlement.

Chapter 15
Assessment of William Allen

In an obituary in the Notices of the Astronomical Society Allen was described as 'an original member of the Astrological Society and a distinguished Professor of Experimental Philosophy at Guy's Hospital and The Royal Institute of Great Britain. His taste for astronomy was evinced by his elegant private observations and his extensive astronomical library … he united in a remarkable degree, sound knowledge, suavity of manners and sterling principles and he deservedly possessed the esteem of all who knew him. Such was William Allen whose life was devoted to the best interests of mankind.'

As a close lifelong friend, Thomas Clarkson may be forgiven for having some bias when he declared that 'William Allen is the greatest man in Europe. He does more good than any man living.'[1] However, other contemporaries also spoke highly of him. Jeremy Bentham considered him 'a fine fellow … ardently benevolent and increasingly rich'[2] and to Henry Brougham 'he was a man among a million',[3] although Joseph Lancaster and Robert Owen had reasons to feel differently! To a farm labourer in Lindfield, he was 'the poor man's friend'[4] and, in 1953, Helena Hall, a Lindfield resident, described him as 'the saviour of the people of Lindfield.'[5] Certainly to this day he is remembered in Lindfield with respect and affection. If to David Salmon in 1904 'Allen alone was worth a thousand men in dealing with the difficulties in Borough Road',[6] eighty years later Dickson described Allen as 'a man of wide sympathies and utmost integrity, sober, unassuming and kind.'[7]

For thirty years treasurer of the BFSS, Allen played a significant role in nineteenth century popular education, helping to put the BFSS on a firm financial footing. His work, however, took place largely behind the scenes and so Bartle's statement that 'Allen's role in early nineteenth century education has been almost forgotten except by his Quaker co-religionists and in the records of the BFSS, whilst the names of Robert Owen and Joseph Lancaster are widely known'[8] is hardly surprising.

E. C. Cripps wrote that 'Allen was known to his day and generation as a scientist of distinction.'[9] Writing in 1965 H. Doncaster described him as 'one of the foremost chemists of his time.' Remarkable achievements for someone who had a limited formal education. There is no mention of Allen in Collins *Biographical Dictionary of Scientists* nor in *Chambers Concise Dictionary of Scientists* – presumably only leading scientists warrant inclusion and there have been many claims to fame since Allen's time. However, there is no doubt that Allen championed the cause of pharmacists and, in the words of J. A. Hunt, 'the rapid establishment of the Pharmaceutical Society of Great Britain in 1841 and its public recognition two years later was due in no small measure to the efforts of William Allen elected the first President.'[10] Incidentally, the Concise Dictionary of National Biography 1992 accords him twelve lines!

Plough Court was a gathering ground for all interested in science and philanthropy – Sir Humphrey Davy, Sir Astley Cooper, Joseph Lancaster, Robert Owen, William Wilberforce, Elizabeth Fry, Thomas Clarkson, Sir Thomas Fowell Buxton and Samuel Hoare. Through campaigning and political interests, Allen associated with men such as Lord Brougham, Jeremy Bentham and Joseph Fox and he became acquainted with royalty, especially the Dukes of Sussex and Kent.

Fayle's book is entitled *The Spitalfields Genius*. Perhaps influenced by this book title, the bicentenary number of *Guy's Hospital Gazette*, published in 1926, also refers to him as the Spitalfields Genius. Was Allen a person of exceptional ability especially of a highly original kind? Interestingly, when Fayle described Allen as a genius in 1884, he quoted Thomas Carlyle's definition: 'Genius means transcendent capacity for taking trouble first of all.' Certainly in this sense of the word Allen qualified. He was a painstaking and prolific correspondent (it is understandable that his comment when the Penny Postage Bill was carried in 1840 was that 'This is indeed a grand measure'). He supervised every detail of projects such as the Spitalfields Soup Society and the Lindfield Allotments and he attended numerous Committee Meetings even in old age. He founded and edited at least three periodicals – *The Philanthropist*, *The Inquirer* and the *Lindfield Reporter and Philanthropist*. He was an astute businessman, founding the successful firm of Allen and Hanburys.

Fayle's conclusion was that although Allen laboured hard for the abolition of slavery, the cause will always more readily be associated with the names of Clarkson, Wilberforce, Fowell Buxton, and Macaulay. It was the same with prison reform, linked with John Howard and Elizabeth Fry. However, his name should be associated with three great schemes which have done so much to alter the condition of the country – the BFSS one of the driving forces in securing universal education for the poor; the Lanark Concern which led to a social 'revolution' amongst the manufacturing hands (in their living conditions), and his 'Colonies' and general efforts to improve the condition of agricultural labourers. This ties in with Perry's description of him as a pioneer of rural education, housing and land settlement. Writing in 1935, Perry's praise is almost on a par with that of Allen's Victorian biographers. With reference to the Lindfield Schools, he wrote: 'This was a system of education very far in advance of his own – its like was not to be found anywhere in the southern counties of England at that time. It was free and in the place given to Arts and Crafts in the curriculum it was completely modern.' [11] Allen appears to have put some of his own finances into the Lindfield Schools of Industry. However, his plan for District Schools did not come to fruition: more than time and the financial efforts of a few people were needed. To some extent the Lindfield experiments were the pet projects of an old man. It is a pity that there is no record of what the children did when they left school. Were they able to use their skills? In urban areas there may have been more scope with apprenticeship opportunities. The later nineteenth century saw a decline in the significance of Schools of Industry, as increasing mechanisation meant that it was not easy for them to make a profit.

Criticisms of his allotment schemes have been made in an earlier chapter. A gradual improvement in the economic situation and the development of alternative sources of work were as important in improving the position of the agricultural labourer, if not more so, as any allotment crop yields. But whatever the drawbacks, the Lindfield allotments were a very real attempt to address the problems of the rural poor. His enthusiasm could mean an over simplistic, over optimistic approach but no one can doubt the sincerity of his efforts. By 1850 allotments were becoming widely recognised as parcels of land to be cultivated by the labourer in his spare time, for the provision of food for himself and his dependants. Fayle wrote: 'I have been unable to make out how it was that William Allen's name alone came to be associated with the 'Colony' – unless he bought up the place?' [12] This was not true. A heriot – money payment to the lord on the death of his tenant, was paid to the Lord of the Manor of South Malling by John Smith's son, John Abel Smith, in 1842.[13] Although Allen mentioned John Smith and the Earl of Chichester in the articles he wrote, inevitably more attention was paid to the editor of the articles. He was also the man on the spot when it came to inspecting the allotments. It was Allen's enthusiasm, drive and his ability to secure the support of friends, that advanced activity in Lindfield. Thus it is not surprising that, then and now, Allen alone is recognised as the great Lindfield benefactor.

Allen showed enormous perseverance and industry in carrying out his humanitarian work, travelling widely in Britain and Europe. He was prepared to present his views even when he anticipated a negative response: 'In an interview with Lord John Russell, I gave him *The Lindfield Reporter*, containing my article on Religious Persecution, telling him at the same time, that I supposed we should not agree upon that subject. He received it very kindly.'[14] It is an interesting reflection on present day society that, whereas Allen's Victorian biographers were full of eulogies about his benevolent good deeds, today we are more cautious. Bartle expressed this well: 'The kind of philanthropy and piety he represented is no longer widely appreciated. The social attitudes he expressed seem too rooted in their period and their class, his humility and apparent mildness somewhat self-deceiving. His cultivation of the great and influential – even from the best of motives – ill accords with his insistence that the poor and socially deprived should accept their station in life.'[15]

The authors of *Through a City Archway* made a different criticism: 'It was perhaps one of life's minor tragedies that his Quakerism prevented William Allen from going more into general society.'[16] They also found it strange that he showed no apparent interest in art, music and literature. There are no diary references to the musical or literary giants of the time with the exception of a quote from Dr Johnson. However, the authors thought that it was probably sheer lack of time and energy rather than because Allen had a narrow religious outlook. It may also be due to the limitations of his severely edited diaries, as there is little reference to any leisure pursuits apart from a visit to Loddidge's Nursery in 1822. 'We all went to Loddidge's Nursery to see the camellias which are now in full bloom and very beautiful! There is quite a forest of them: his hot houses are, perhaps, the most capacious in the world: one of them is forty feet high: in this there is a banana tree which reaches to the top.'[17]

David Hitchin's observations are interesting:

'The authors of *Through a City Archway* should not have considered it strange that Allen showed no apparent interest in art, music and literature. Almost from the beginning the Discipline forbade music. By the 1860s some children at a Quaker boarding school in Lewes went to a music teacher over the road, but even in the 1880s many Quakers prominent in charity work refused to attend fund-raising concerts. The books of discipline strongly discouraged the reading of fiction. Alfred Waterhouse, the architect of Quaker origins who designed the Natural History Museum, only turned to architecture because his parents forbade him the frivolity of life as a painter. Quakers were narrow and odd, but Allen no more so than most. Many Friends of earlier generations questioned this narrowness, and from around the 1860s fewer and fewer observed it strictly, but it was not until 1937 that the Society formally recognised and encouraged art, music and literature.'

Allen was not uncultured – he obviously had a great knowledge of the Bible and could read Greek and Latin. Even the unedited diaries, intended as a diary record of his thoughts and strivings to achieve a successful life as a practising Christian, may not have revealed more about his cultural interests. The editing of the diaries has meant that some areas of his life cannot be fully explored. It would have been of interest to learn more about his relationship with the Scottish philosopher James Mill, who produced many articles for *The Philanthropist* and co-operated with Allen in promoting a large number of reforms. Mill responded to the attacks of The National Society. His review, republished as *Schools for All in Preference to Schools for Churchmen only*, had an important influence on radical opinion. There is no reference to Allen's relationship with Francis Place or Jeremy Bentham and his followers, who all had a more secular approach to mass education for the poor, while Allen supported his friend Joseph Fox in the view that the Bible should be the sole reading book in BFSS schools. 'Allen's contributions to popular education can not be ignored. Without his efforts on its behalf, the BFSS would surely not have survived – though Allen must share some responsibility for the narrow and mechanical characteristics of the British System in its earlier years.'[18] It is easy, with hindsight, to criticise the lack of a scientific emphasis in all the schools for the poor, both BFSS and National Society schools, but this perhaps underrates the contemporary problem of providing some elementary education for all, which both Societies, assisted from 1833 by growing government finance and supervision, did achieve. Allen was also involved in the BFSS overseas projects, and although they were criticised by some contemporaries when there was so much to do at home, they were often successful, as in the West Indies.

An attempt has been made to place William Allen in his contemporary society. He was neither an innovator nor a genius but, to quote his own words, 'can humbly say in the multitude of things which harness the mind, the main object is the good of others.'[19] Allen was one of the most versatile and influential Quakers of his generation – one of a group of philanthropists who worked hard to deal with the difficult social issues of the day – emancipation of slaves, education for the masses, religious tolerance for minorities, prison reform – to name but a few of the causes addressed by what he termed 'Friends of Humanity'.

*Portrait of William Allen,
from a photograph of an engraving by P. Elie Bovet of Geneva, 1823.
(Library of the Religious Society of Friends in Britain.)*

Bibliography

Life of William Allen with Selections from his Correspondence. In three volumes, edited by L. Bradshaw. C. Gilpin. 1846.

Memoirs of William Allen F.R.S. J. Sherman. 1857.

William Allen; His Life and Labours. Printed for the Tract Association of the Religious Society of Friends. 1865. Reprinted by the Society in 1875 to commemorate the Jubilee of the Lindfield British School in 1875.

Glimpses of our Ancestors in Sussex. Gleanings in E & W Sussex, 2nd series. C. Fleet. 1883.

The Spitalfields Genius: The Story of William Allen. J. Fayle. 1884.

William Allen. D. Salmon. 1905

Memorials of Christine Majolier Alsop. Compiled by M. Braithwaite. 1881.

The Life of William Allen – Spitalfields Genius. Helena Hall. 1953.

Through a City Archway – The Story of Allen and Hanburys. D. Chapman-Huston and E. C. Cripps. 1954.

The Story of Quakerism. E. Vipont.

Annals of the Congregational Church at Lindfield. N. Caplan.

History of Sussex. Vol.1. Horsfield.

The Life and Ideas of Robert Owen. A. L. Morton.

Wilberforce. J. Pollock.

Joseph Lancaster The Poor Child's Friend. J. Taylor.

The Chronicles of Fleetwood House. A. J. Shirren.

Catalogue of Prints and Drawings in the British Museum. Div. 1. Political and Personal Satires. Vol.X. 1820-27. M. D. George.

Society and Economy in Modern Britain 1700-1850. R. Brown.

The Age of Caricature. Satirical Prints in the Reign of George III. D. Donald 1996.

Life of James Mill. A. Bain.

The Bruising Apothecary – Images of Pharmacy and Medicine in Caricature. K. Arnold Forster & N. Tallis.

Access to History Themes: The Industrialisation of Britain 1780-1914. P. Chapple.

Sussex Schools in 18c. J. M. Caffyn.

The Mendips. A. W. Coysh, E. J. Mason, V. Waite. 1962.

At the Sign of the Plough. 275 Years of Allen and Hanburys and the British Pharmaceutical Industry 1715 – 1990. G. Tweedale.

Articles

'A 19c. Social Experiment'. W. H. G. Armytage.

'William Allen The Educational Record – Proceedings of the BFSS'. 1905.

'William Allen – A Profile'. G. E.Trease.

'Friends of Humanity'. L. H. Doncaster. 1965.

'A Brief History of the Allotment Movement'. P. L. Grier.

'William Allen – Friend of Humanity – His Role in 19c. Popular Education'. G. F. Bartle. History of Education Society Bulletin no.50. 1992.

'The Theory and Practice of Pre-Vocational Education 1780-1840. M. Dick. Education and Employment – Initiatives and Experiences 1780 to the Present. History of Education Society.

Notes and References

Preface and Introduction

1. Johnsonian Miscellanies Vol.II, p.309.
2. Allen left no immediate family. Francis Clayton used this expression when writing to George William Allen of Dorking about the 1846 diary editors. The destruction on the original diaries caused consternation amongst other branches of the family.
3. James Mill. 1773-1836. Scottish philosopher, historian and economist – a friend of Jeremy Bentham. He co-operated with Allen in the production of *The Philanthropist*. Topics included education of poor, penny clubs for clothing, employment of poor women, attempts to provide civilisation in Africa, and prison reform.
4. Benthamites – followers of Jeremy Bentham, 1748-1832, English philosopher, economist and social reformer. Pioneer of Utilitarianism – the aim of all actions and legislation should be 'the greatest happiness of the greatest number'.
5. Stephen Grellet, 1773-1855. He was of French origin but emigrated to New York in 1795. The following year he became a Quaker and in 1798 a minister. He made four visits to Europe and accompanied William Allen on his journey to Russia.
6. In 1652 the term 'Friends in the Truth' came into use. The name Society of Friends arose much later.
7. *Journal of George Fox*, p.65.
8. *First Among Friends*, pp.121,192. L. Ingle. OUP 1994.
9. The Oath of Abjuration required suspected Roman Catholics to take an oath renouncing papal authority and the doctrine of transubstantiation. In the 17c. it was used against Quakers who took the commandment of Jesus to 'swear not at all' literally.
10. C. Fleet. Glimpses of our Ancestors in Sussex, 1883. 2nd series, p.79.
11. The 1666 Toleration Act allowed legally recognised sects to conduct their own religious worship within certain limitations. Dissenting ministers were recognised provided they subscribed to all 39 Articles. Quakers were allowed to affirm the Oath of Allegiance or Supremacy. Affirming meant the solemn declaration by a person who conscientiously objected to taking an oath.
12. The Test and Corporation Acts passed in the reign of Charles II were designed to prevent anyone who was not an Anglican communicant from holding the most important state offices or being members of local corporations. Protestant Dissenters were later freed from penalties by an Annual Act of Indemnity. The Acts were not repealed until 1828.
13. In the 17c. and 18c. an apothecary was not only a practising dispenser and

druggist; he was also responsible for prescribing remedies, so that apprenticeship to him was a recognised way of entry into the medical profession. Until the end of the 18c. druggists and chemists largely confined their business to wholesaling, compounding and retail sales. Chemists were dealers in chemicals. Druggists dealt in drugs of animal and vegetable origin. The early 19c. saw a rise in the status of the druggist and chemist to that of the profession of pharmacy. In 1815 the right to buy, compound, dispense and sell drugs and medicines by wholesale or retail was established by Act of Parliament. There was growing competition with the apothecary who still held exclusive right to dispense the physician's prescription.

14. Dr Fothergill prescribed simple drugs instead of complicated mixtures. He stressed the importance of a wholesome diet, cleanliness and fresh air especially in cases of consumption.
15. John Dalton conducted experiments to determine the simple proportions in which elements combined.
16. With Barry's retirement in 1856, the business became known as Allen and Hanburys.

Chapter 1: Early Life and Education

1. Dame schools were opened by elderly women and some men. At worst little more than child minding took place. At best, some basic education was provided. The fee for reading was 1d. or 2d. a week, writing as well – 3d. or 4d. a week.
2. *Life of William Allen with selections from his correspondence.* C. Gilpin, 1846 (henceforth cited as *Allen*), Vol.I, p.128.
3. Ibid. *Allen,* Vol.I, p.46.
4. *Through a City Archway,* Chapman-Huston and Cripps, p.282.
5. *Allen*, Vol.I, p.27.
6. Ibid, p.49.
7. Ibid, p.51.
8. Ibid, p.127.
9. Ibid, p.153.
10. Ibid, p.3.
11. Ibid, pp.5-6
12. Bryan Higgins, 1737-1820, a chemist and physician who gave lectures on Science in Greek Street, Soho, London.
13. *Allen*, Vol.I, pp.31-32.
14. Ibid, p.5.
15. Ibid, p.26.
16. Ibid, p.141.

17. Ibid, p.11.
18. The Quaker Calendar. Quakers objected to using the names of days (Sunday to Saturday) and months (January to August) which derived from heathen gods or goddesses, and they employed numbers instead. From 1752 Quakers referred to all months by their number. The American practice of putting the month before the day when giving a date was also widely used by British Friends.
19. *Allen*, Vol.I, p.143.
20. *Allen*, Vol.II, p.200.
21. *Through a City Archway*, p.91.
22. *Allen*, Vol.III, pp.312-313. The spelling is now Gravelye.
23. *Allen*, Vol.I, p.26.
24. Ibid, p.42.
25. Nitrous Oxide, or laughing gas, was first studied systematically by Humphrey Davy.
26. *Allen*, Vol.I, pp.47-48.
27. Letter from Humphrey Davy. *Allen*, Vol.I, p.127.
28. *Through a City Archway*, no.14, p.286.
29. *Allen*, Vol.I, p.59.
30. Ibid, p.63.
31. Ibid, p.60.
32. Ibid, pp.111-112.
33. For more details see: *At the Sign of the Plough. Allen and Hanburys and the British Pharmaceutical Industry 1715-1990*, G. Tweedale, pp.34-56. *Through a City Archway* and material in Allen and Hanburys Archive.
34. *At the Sign of the Plough*, G. Tweedale, p.56.

Chapter 2: William Allen's Humanitarian Interests

1. Max Weber – *The Protestant Ethic and the Spirit of Capitalism*. Allen and Unwin, 1930.
2. Ian Bradley – quoted in *The Upper Classes*, J. Scott, p.65. Macmillan, 1980.
3. David McClelland – *The Achieving Society*, 1961. Princeton University Press. For a further discussion see *Society and Economy in Britain 1700 – 1850*, R. Brown, pp.210-213
4. *The Philanthropist II*, p.175 – a quarterly journal which Allen edited from 1810-1817.
5. *Allen*, Vol.I, p.131
6. Ibid, p.262.

7. Ibid, pp.172-173.
8. Ibid, p.175.
9. Ibid, p.228.
10. Ibid, p.340.

Chapter 3: Opposition to the Slave Trade

1. *Allen*, Vol.I, pp.4,7.
2. Ibid, p.15.
3. Ibid, p.82.
4. Ibid, p.179.
5. Ibid, p.7.
6. Ibid, p.180.
7. Ibid, p.118.
8. Memoirs of C. M. Alsop, 1881, p.69.

Chapter 4: Allen as a National and 'International' Figure

1. *Allen*, Vol.I, p.283. Johann Heinrich Pestalozzi was interested in the education of poor children. His ideas for a wide curriculum which included swimming, games and music and his belief in a 'friendly relationship between teacher and pupil' had a large influence on educational thought.
2. Fayle, *The Spitalfields Genius*, 1881, p.152.
3. *Allen*, Vol.I, pp.375-380, Vol.II, p.20.
4. *Allen*, Vol.II, p.363.
5. Ibid, Vol.I, pp.194-201.
6. Ibid, Vol.II, p.6, Letter to J. Forster.
7. Ibid, Vol.I, pp.465-468.
8. Fayle, *The Spitalfields Genius*, 1881, p.92.
9. *Allen*, Vol.II, pp.240, 257-262.
10. Ibid, p.264-265.
11. Ibid, p.285.
12. Letter from archive collection, Friends Library, Euston.

Chapter 5: Marriages and Family Life

1. *Allen*, Vol.I, p.27.
2. Ibid, p.29.
3. Ibid, p.65.
4. *Allen*, Vol.II, p.437.

5. Original letters (first two by same correspondent) are in the Friends Library, Euston. 17, 38, 39.
6. *Allen*, Vol.III, p.208.
7. *Through a City Archway*, p.108.
8. *Allen*, Vol.III, p.352.
9. *Memorials of C. M. Alsop*, 1881, p.41.
10. Ibid, p.67.
11. Ibid, p.69.
12. Ibid, p.70.
13. Ibid, p.59.
14. Ibid, pp.71-72.
15. Fayle, *The Spitalfields Genius*, 1881, p.198.
16. *Memorials of C. M. Alsop*, 1881, p.117.
17. *Allen*, Vol.III, p.437.

Chapter 6:
Political and Personal Satire and Brief Description of 1827 Caricatures

1. The Queen's Affair – The Prince Regent had secretly married Mrs. Fitzherbert, a divorced Catholic, in 1785. Ten years later, under pressure from George III and in the hope of clearing his debts, he committed bigamy by marrying Princess Caroline of Brunswick. When he became King in 1820, he sought dissolution of his marriage to Caroline by Act of Parliament. The public enquiry which followed seriously damaged the reputation of the monarchy as did Caroline's attempt to force her way into Westminster Abbey when the Coronation took place.
2. *The Age of Caricature*, D. Donald, pp.184,198.
3. Extracts from a letter from D. Donald, October 27th 2000. p.198.
4. *Catalogue of Political and Personal Satires*, M. D. George, Vol.X, p.711.

Chapter 7: Contemporary Educational Views

1. *An Account of Charity Schools lately erected*, 1708.
2. *Joseph Lancaster The Poor Child's Friend*, J. Taylor, p.61.
3. Hannah More – *The Mendips*, A. W. Coysh, E. J. Mason and V. Waite, p.96.
4. Ibid, p.99.

Chapter 8:
Allen's Involvement with Lancaster, Owen and Fleetwood House

1. *Allen*, Vol.I, p.94.
2. Ibid, p.112.

3. Ibid – letter to T. W. Smith, p.109.
4. Extract from a copy of a draft letter written by Allen. BFSS File 008.
5. *Allen*, Vol.I, p.132.
6. Ibid, p.153.
7. Ibid, p.191 (abridged).
8. BFSS File 008.
9. Quoted in *His Role in 19c. Popular Education*, G. F. Bartle, p.18.
10. *Allen*, Vol.III, p.10.
11. *Allen*, Vol.I, p.244.
12. Ibid, p.344.
13. *Allen*, Vol.II, p.226.
14. Ibid, pp.374-375.
15. Owen. *Life of Robert Owen written by himself*, 1867, p.141.
16. Ibid, p.235.
17. Ibid, p.95.
18. *Through a City Archway*, no.24, p.296.
19. *Allen*, Vol.II, p.407.
20. *Chronicles of Fleetwood House*, A. J. Shirren, p.164.

Chapter 10: The Lindfield Connection – Why Lindfield?

1. *Abstract of Returns relative to the Expense and Maintenance of the Poor*, 1803.
2. C. Fleet. *Glimpses of our Ancestors in Sussex*. 2nd series, p.197.
3. Ibid, p.196.
4. *Victoria County History*, Vol.II, p.40.
5. J. M. Caffyn, *Sussex Schools in 18c.*, pp.191-192.
6. John Chater's return to the Registration Commission quoted in *Extracts from the Annals of the Congregational Church*, C. Caplan, p.15.

Chapter 11:
The Establishment of Schools of Industry and a Boarding School in Lindfield

1. *Allen*, Vol.II, p.384. This was not the first time Lindfield residents had been criticised for their conservatism. A 1658 Report on the Survival of Catholic pieties and support stated: "They have yet in this diocese in many places images hidden up and other popish ornaments, ready to be sett *[sic]* up for Mass again within 24 hours warning; as in the town of Battel and in the parish of Lindfield where they be yet very blind and superstitious." *The Clergy and the Elizabethan Settlement in the Diocese of Chichester.* T. J. McCann, p.100.

2. Bartle, *History of Education Society Bulletin* No.50, 1992, p.24.
3. *Glimpses of our Ancestors in Sussex*, 2nd Series, pp.201-203.
4. *The Theory and Practice of Pre-Vocational Education 1780-1840*, M. Dick, pp.1-5; *Education and Employment Initiatives and Experiences 1780 to the Present; History of Education Society Bulletin,* 1988.
5. C. M. Alsop, pp.89-91.
6. *Allen*, Vol.III, p.233.
7. Ibid, p.254.
8. Ibid, p.267.
9. Ibid, p.274.
10. Ibid, pp.181-182.
11. Ibid, p.231.
12. Ibid, p.289.
13. Ibid, p.203.
14. Ibid, p.293.
15. Ibid, p.405.

Chapter 14: The Lindfield Allotments

1. P. L. Grier, *A Brief History of the Allotment Movement,* p.2c
2. Ibid, p.3c.
3. As recorded in *The Times* obituary notice of William Marquess of Cholmondeley.
4. Fayle mentions a letter he received from Lord Chichester informing him that neither he nor his father who died in 1826 had any pecuniary interest in the Colony. *The Spitalfields Genius*, p.17.
5. Helena Hall, *Life of William Allen – Spitalfields Genius*, p.118; Alsop, p.71.
6. Fleet, op.cit. Vol.II, pp.198-201.
7. Ibid, p.201.
8. *The Lindfield Reporter*, Feb.1835, Vol.II, no.2, pp.20-21. *The Lindfield Reporter* was first published in 1835 but appears to have replaced earlier magazines entitled *The Philanthropist* and *Inquirer.*
9. Fleet, op.cit. Vol.II, p.198.
10. Fayle, op.cit. p.7.
11. Armytage, *A 19c. Social Experiment.*
12. Fayle, op.cit. p.13.
13. *The Lindfield Reporter*, Feb.1835, Vol.II, pp.19,20.
14. *The Lindfield Reporter*, 1837, pp.122-123.

15. *Through a City Archway*, Appendix no.23, pp.294-296.
16. *Allen*, Vol.III, p.23.
17. Ibid, p.188.
18. Ibid, p.233.
19. Ibid, p.189.
20. Sydney Smith, 1771-1845, Canon at St Paul's, educated at Winchester and New College Oxford. He published the Plumley Letters in defence of Catholic Emancipation, 1807. Foston is near York.
21. *Through a City Archway*, no.24, pp.293-294.
22. Fayle, *The Spitalfields Genius*, p.15.
23. Ibid, p.16.
24. *Victoria County History*, Vol.II, p.208.

Chapter 15: Assessment of William Allen

1. Quoted in L. H. Doncaster, *Friends of Humanity*, 1965, p.8.
2. Bentham to A. Burr, Jan.19th 1811, *The Correspondence of J.B.*, VIII Ed. S. Conway, p.94.
3. A letter to the Duke of Bedford, quoted in D. Salmon, p.21.
4. Fleet, pp.198-201.
5. Helena Hall, *Life of William Allen – Spitalfields Genius*, p.11.
6. *Joseph Lancaster*, D. Salmon, 1904, p.39.
7. *Teacher Extraordinary Joseph Lancaster*, M. Dickson, p.110.
8. *William Allen*, G. F. Bartle, *History of Education Society Bulletin* no.50, 1992, p.25.
9. *The Pharmaceutical Journal*, E. C. Cripps, 1943.
10. *The Pharmaceutical Journal*, J. A. Hunt, 1994.
11. Article in *The Sussex Country Life* Nov.1935, R. Perry.
12. Fayle, *The Spitalfields Genius*, p.8.
13. West Sussex Record Office, Lindfield (Add MS 22,337).
14. *Allen*, Vol.III, p.416.
15. *William Allen*, G. F. Bartle, *History of Education Society Bulletin* no.50, 1992, p.25.
16. *Through a City Archway*, pp.91-93.
17. Ibid, p.279 no.6.
18. G. F. Bartle, op.cit. p.25.
19. *Allen*, Vol.I, p.143.

Index

	Page
Abolition of Slave Trade Act	36
African Institution	41,43,75
Agriculture, Board of	33
Alexander I	20,43,47,48,49,50,79
Allen, Job	20,22
Allen, Margaret	20,22
Allen, Mary	20,21,46,52,56

Allen, William (1770-1843) –
chronology	20,21
birth and early education	22
family tree	23
influence of mother	25,26
clerkship at Plough Court	22
self education	25
influence of Quakerism	25,29
scientific interests	28-34
first President of the Pharmaceutical Society of Great Britain	21,34
humanitarian interests –	
Spitalfields hand loom weavers	39
soup kitchen	38,39
Association for relief of the poor	39
penal reform	41
juvenile delinquency	41
visit to Newgate prison	41
opposition to the slave trade	42-45
the African Institution	43
Declaration against slave trade at the Congress of Vienna	43
the Abolition lobby at the Congress of Verona	43
Anti Slavery Society	44
Visits abroad	46-51
conditions of travel	46,47
marriages and family life	
Mary Hamilton	20,52,66
daughter Mary	20,21,46,52,56
Charlotte Hanbury	20,52,53,56,66
Grizell Birkbeck	52-56
daily life	56-58

caricatures of 1827	60-67
visit to Borough Road School	72
relationship with Joseph Lancaster	74,75
treasurer for BFSS	74,76
relationship with Robert Owen	76-79
partnership of New Lanark Mills	76
Fleetwood House Boarding School	79
The Lindfield schools	90-100
Allen's personal involvement	101
Lindfield boarding school	102-105
plan for district schools	106-110
Lindfield schools 1832-2000	111-114
Lindfield allotments	116
pamphlet Colonies at Home	116
how the allotments were set up	117
the cottages	118-120
the tenants agreement	123
future developments	124
plan of a cottage and farmyard	125
the 'Colony' of America	126
publication of Allen's Schemes	129-132
success of the allotments	134-138
demolition of allotment cottages	139
local road names	139
death	21
Anglican Society	70
Anti Slavery Society	44
Apothecaries Act	34
Astronomical Society	33,140
Babington, Dr. William	29
Barclay, Charles	39
Barry, John Thomas	20,33
Bavaria, King of	51
Bedford, Peter	39,41,58,101
Bell, Jacob	34
Bellers, John	101
Bentham, Jeremy	8,36,69,75,76,140,141,144

Benthamites	8,36
Berzelius, Professor Jons Jacob	29
Bevan, Joseph Gurney	20,22,29,30,33
Birkbeck, Grizell	21,52,53,54,55,56,57,60,62,64,66,79
Board of Agriculture	33
Borough Road School	72,74,75,79,101
Bradley, Ian	37
Bradshaw, Lucy	8,57,58,62
British and Foreign School Society (BFSS)	48,72,74,75,76,102,140,141,144
Brougham, Lord Henry	36,57,58,69,129,140,141
Buxton, Thomas Fowell	41,42,44,141
Canning, George	47
Capital Punishment, Society for Abolition	41
Capital Punishment, Society for Diminishing	39
Chichester, 2nd Earl of	21,87,91,117,118,142
Chichester, 3rd Earl of	91,111,117,136
Christian Observer	36
Church Rates	28
Clapham Sect	36
Clarendon Code	16
Clarkson, Thomas	42,43,44,45,50,52,140,141
Cobbett, William	38,85
Colonies at Home	116,118,126,129,132
Congress of Verona	43,49
Conventicle Act	16
Cooper, Astley	29,30,141
Corder, Susanna	8,54,58,62,79,80
Corston, William	101,117
Crawford, William	41
Cruikshank, George	59
Cruikshank, Robert	60,64

Dalton, John	18,29
Dampier, Bishop	68
Davy, Sir Humphrey	20,29,31,141
District Schools	106-110
Dudley, Charles	39
Dunn, Henry	76
Edgeworth, Maria	133
Education Act	111,112
Emancipation of Slaves Act	36
Five-Acre Farms at Lindfield	131,132
Five-Mile Act	16
Fleetwood House Boarding School	79,101
Fox, George	15,17,54
Fox, Joseph	33,74,75,141,144
Fry, Elizabeth	20,41,46,51,52,101,141
Galitzin, Prince	50
General Enclosure Act	117
Geological Society	20,33
Gillray, James	59
Grellet, Stephen	10,46,48,49
Grubb, John	53
Gurney, Joseph John	41,42,98
Hamilton, Mary	20,52,66
Hanbury, Charlotte	20,52,53,56,66
Hanbury, Cornelius	20,21,41,52,56,57,132
Hanbury, Daniel Bell	21
Hanbury, William Allen	21,52,57
Hoare, Samuel	141
Hogarth, William	59
Holland, Henry, 3rd baron	36,69

Horsley, Samuel	69
Howard, Luke	20,33
Institution, African	41,43,75
Institution, Royal Jennerian	31
Jenner, Dr.	33
Jennerian Institution, Royal	31
Johnson, Rev.	120,122
Juvenile delinquency	41,74
Kent, Duke of	51,53,141
Lancaster, Joseph	59,69,70,72,74,75,79,93,140,141
Lancasterian Society	72
Lindfield Reporter (or Philanthropic Magazine)	97,100,103,106,132,141,142
Lindfield Schools set up by Allen	90-105,142
Linnaean Society	33
Locke, John	101
Macaulay, Lachary	36
Macaulay, Stephen	44,141
Majolier (Alsop), Christine	56,57,58,98,100,118
McClelland, David	37
Meeting for Sufferings	18,20,42
Mennonites	47
Mildred, Samuel	20,33
Mill, James	8,144
Mill, John Stuart	117
More, Hannah	70,71,97
Morgan case	39

National School Society	70
New Lanark	20,76,78,79
O'Connor, Feargus	117
Owen, Robert	20,59,69,76,78,79,101,117,129,140,141
Pelham, Thomas, 2nd Earl of Chichester	21,87,91,117,118,142
Pelham, Henry, 3rd Earl of Chichester	91,111,117,136
Penal Code	39
Penn, William	16
Penny Banks	39
Pepys, W. H.	29
Pestalozzi, Johann Heinrich	46,79,151
Pharmaceutical Society of Great Britain	21,34,141
Philanthropist, The	8,20,38,39,46,75,141,144
Phillips, William	39
Place, Francis	69,75,101,144
Plan for Diminishing the Poor Rates	129
Plough Court	20,22,29,30,33,39,56,57,141
Poor Law Amendment Act	129,138
Prince Regent	39,59,152
Prussia, King of	47,58
Quakerism	15
growth of Quakers	15
faith	16
organisation	17
peace testimony	17
education	18
involvement in Trade & Industry	18
pressure group for reform	18
Reeve, Clara	101
Romilly, Sir Samuel	39
Rowlandson, Thomas	59

Rural Colonies at Lindfield	123,129
Russell, Lord John	129,142
Select Committee on Emigration	138
Sewell, Rev. F. Hill	112
Sharp, Granville	36,43
Sidmouth, Lord	39
Slave Trade Act, Abolition of	36
Smith, John	21,57,91,118,122,129,131,136,142
Smith, Sydney	134
Society for Abolition of Capital Punishment	41
Society for Diminishing Capital Punishment	39
Somerset Judgement	42
Spain, King and Queen of	51
Speenhamland System	86,118
Spitalfields Local Association for the Poor	26,39
Spitalfields School	26
Spitalfields Soup Society	37,39,141
Stephens, James	36
Stevens, Robert	39
Sunday School Movement	68,69
Sussex, Duke of	129,141
Sweden, King of	58
Tawney, R. H.	37
Trimmer, Sarah	69,70,101
Verona, Congress of	43,49
Victoria, Queen	51
Waldenses	47
Watson, Mary	54
Watson, Rev. Joseph	89
Weber, Max	37

Wellington, Duke of	43,49
Wells, Thomas	112
Whitbread, Samuel	36,69
Wilberforce, William	36,38,42,43,44,50,57,60,70,129,141
Young, Arthur	117,122,123